LET'S GET SERIOUS ABOUT TEACHING CHILDREN TO WRITE

Jerral R. Hicks

UNIVERSITY
PRESS OF
AMERICA

Lanham • New York • London

Copyright © 1993 by
University Press of America®, Inc.
4720 Boston Way
Lanham, Maryland 20706

3 Henrietta Street
London WC2E 8LU England

Library of Congress Cataloging-in-Publication Data

Hicks, Jerral R.
Let's get serious about teaching children to write / by Jerral R. Hicks.
p.   cm.
Includes bibliographical references and index.
1. English language—Composition and exercises—Study and teaching
(Elementary)—United States.   2. Curriculum planning—United
States.   I. Title.
LB1576.H345   1993   372.6'23'044—dc20   92–35460 CIP

ISBN 0–8191–8945–6 (paper : alk. paper)

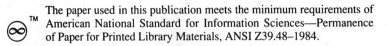

The paper used in this publication meets the minimum requirements of
American National Standard for Information Sciences—Permanence
of Paper for Printed Library Materials, ANSI Z39.48–1984.

TO:

Grace Payne
Sandra Hicks
Clifton and Zella Mae Hicks

TABLE OF CONTENTS

PREFACE

During the 1960s, educators began to voice concern about Johnny's poor reading abilities. By the end of the decade, countless studies had indicated that Johnny's reading skills were in a sad state and, even worse, were continuing to deteriorate. A nation-wide effort was mounted to address this concern. Conferences, seminars, and meetings at all levels searched for ways to reverse this trend. Johnny's reading skills had to improve! Reading was moved to the forefront as a top priority in American schools. More instructional time was provided for reading in elementary and secondary schools, and new programs were developed and implemented. At the college level, teacher training programs were revamped so students received more direct instruction in the teaching of reading. At the graduate level, the reading specialist program and certificate were created.

And what was done about writing during the 1960s? It was largely ignored. Although some research began to focus on children's writing in the 1960s, it wasn't until the 1970s that educators began to realize that children's writing skills were also in a sad state—even worse than their reading abilities. As one educator said, "If you think Johnny's reading is poor, you should see his writing!" Why didn't we realize this earlier and respond to this problem? It seems so obvious that a child who is a poor reader will be even a worse writer.

A concerted effort to reassess the priority on writing and respond to the poor writing skills of American youth didn't fully materialize until the early 1980s. Or so it seemed. Improving children's writing skills was identified as a high priority in new language arts programs, and curriculum guides delineated countless writing skills. As with reading before, conferences, seminars, and meetings at various levels were held to define the elements and direction critical to effective writing programs. And what impact did all this have on students' writing skills? Through the 1980s, not much. Studies have indicated—and continue to indicate, little or no improvement in most cases.

Why haven't we realized greater improvement in the writing skills of American youth? Much of the answer, I believe, lies in the failure to make a serious commitment of resources to writing in public schools and to the training of teachers. In public schools, writing instruction is usually still limited to a portion of the language arts block, and in higher education there has been little, or in many cases, no change in the preparation of teachers to teach writing! While reading specialists are quite common, how many have heard of a writing specialist? How about a literacy specialist who gives equal attention to reading and writing?

Why haven't we made a serious commitment to writing? The answer likely varies. It may result from a lack of understanding about the complex nature of writing, a failure to realize the importance of writing, a failure to realize the amount of time needed to become an effective writer, or, more likely, a combination of these and other factors.

We need to get serious about teaching children to write. We've already designated the significant improvement of children's writing skills as a goal. Now we need to understand the importance and the difficulty of the task, then make a **real** commitment of the necessary resources to achieve our goal.

Foremost among my goals in this work is that it will result in more effective writing programs in our schools. Chapter 1 focuses on the importance of writing and its status in our schools today. Chapter 2 presents an in-depth examination of the nature of writing, why it is difficult, the stages of development, and the purposes and types of writing. Chapter 3 is a presentation of pertinent research and of my observations that provide direction for an effective strategy and teaching techniques. In Chapter 4, the characteristics of an effective writing program and a strategy for developing a writing program are described. Chapter 5 focuses on developing children's appreciation of writing and setting the stage for writing in the classroom, and describes numerous writing activities that I have observed to be effective. In Chapter 6, a writing curriculum is presented for kindergarten through grade six, including the types of materials, rhetorical modes, concepts and skills, and the persistent writing problems of children that commonly need special attention.

CHAPTER 1: PUTTING WRITING IN PERSPECTIVE

Of the four modes of communication—listening, speaking, reading, and writing—writing is the slowest to develop and the most difficult to perform. Writing abilities are invariably less well developed than reading abilities. Given the marginal reading skills of many students, it's no surprise, then, that teacher observations and research findings indicate serious deficiencies in many children's writing abilities.

Likewise, the writing skills of many of us adults are marginally adequate. Like many children, many of us adults dislike writing and lack confidence in our writing abilities. When confronted with a writing task, we often procrastinate, dread getting started. We even avoid writing when we can. For example, when given the choice, graduate students will nearly always complete an additional six semester hours of coursework rather than write a thesis for a masters degree. And in daily communications, it's so easy to pick up the phone. Writing just takes too much time!

And yet, we have no choice. We **must** teach children how to write. The ability to write is not only vital to each individual from a personal standpoint, it is essential in the world of business and to the leadership our nation provides in the world.

The Historical Impact of Writing

If writing is so difficult, if it is so unpleasant, why did anyone bother to invent it? For thousands of years, knowledge was passed on from one generation to the next through customs, rituals, superstitions, folktales, and myths. Memory and the spoken word served as the basis for transmitting all information. The amount of knowledge passed on from one generation to the next, then, was limited according to the memories of the elders and those individuals and groups who listened. The elders discovered that they sometimes forgot, and that those who listened didn't always remember. A need to communicate more completely and reliably became apparent.

Drawings and other mediums began to be used to communicate ideas. But as the desire to transmit ever greater amounts of information grew, it became apparent that drawings were also inadequate. A still more effective means of communicating was needed! Ultimately, a system of symbols was invented for the purpose of representing the sounds in the existing spoken language. When used in combinations according to accepted rules, these symbols enabled users of a common language to communicate through a new medium: Writing! Writers were able to communicate with those in other places, those they could not hear or see.

Writing! Our greatest invention. No other invention has had such profound impact on human development and history. It has allowed us to transmit information across time and space accurately and reliably. We can read the thoughts of someone who lived centuries ago. We can experience the adventure, excitement, and hardship of others in far away places by reading what they have written! We can learn from those who lived long ago through the written record they left behind.

Writing literally made recorded history possible and served as the springboard for modern civilization! How? It enabled us to maintain a record of events and, more importantly, to accumulate knowledge far beyond that which we individually could store and retrieve from memory. Books, newspapers, encyclopedias, libraries, and computer disks provide ways of storing and retrieving much more information than any one person can possibly remember. They are, in essence, our extended brain. While our ability to accumulate knowledge was quite limited before writing, then, it was made virtually limitless with writing. This unlimited ability to accumulate information eventually led to the knowledge base for modern civilization.

But how has this accumulation of knowledge led to modern civilization? First, we need to consider what has fueled this accumulation. There is, of course, our basic struggle for survival. Our on-going efforts to meet our basic needs for food, shelter, spiritual/emotional well-being, protection from various threats to our physical well-being, and our innate curiosity about our world have challenged our intellect. But other animals must also meet most of these same needs in their struggle for survival. Two characteristics that are unique to us, however, apparently provide much of the driving force: our desire to do things more efficiently, and our appreciation for comfort and convenience. As conservers of work, we are constantly trying to figure out how to do things easier, better, and quicker. Just imagine how many times someone has thought, "There's gotta be a better way to do this!" This single thought has led to thousands of inventions, such as the wagon, crossbow, printing press, and railroad. Our appreciation for comfort and convenience has led to countless other inventions, such as the flush toilet, lightbulb, and air conditioner. Writing, then, hasn't just resulted in a more complete record of trivia and events. More importantly, it has also focused on day-to-day problems and how those problems have been solved through invention.

As we have accumulated knowledge and inventions, we have developed and applied science and technology at increasingly complex levels, with each new invention resting on earlier related developments. The invention of the automobile, for example, didn't just require new developments such as gasoline. Hundreds of earlier inventions, such as the wheel, screw, countless developments in metallurgy, and gearing, were adapted to this new, more complex mode of transportation. Without a substantial prior knowledge base, then, there would not have been a Boeing 747, vaccines, supercomputers, an Apollo spaceship, or heart transplants. No individual could have been inventive enough to have developed even one of these and all prior related developments by himself! He had to have access to the related discoveries and inventions of earlier generations. Writing provided access to that knowledge.

Writing, then, served as the portal for more complex thinking and, with the invention of the printing press, greatly accelerated the pace of technological achievements. It is no coincidence that reading materials became much more widely available with the invention of the printing press **during** the Renaissance. Indeed, the Renaissance man was a well-read man. Books were among his most prized possessions. Prior to the printing press, however, the production of books was a painstakingly slow task; each book had to be handwritten. Books were, as a result, relatively scarce. But with the printing press, the potential impact of writing was greatly enhanced. More books began to be published, and, more importantly, more copies of books became available. Coupled with the establishment of universities and their libraries in Europe and then in America, unprecedented strides began to be made in complex, technical thinking. The stage was set for the Industrial Revolution.

The Industrial Revolution brought about major cultural and societal changes. Two hallmarks of modern societies are an advanced level of technical achievement and a relatively fast pace of innovation or change. Tradition, for better or worse, often takes a back seat to technological innovation. Each new generation accomplishes many tasks somewhat differently from the preceding generation.

As societies modernized, they reshaped themselves. How so? The flood of inventions and technical achievements, especially during the 19th and 20th centuries, resulted in revolutionary changes in production, transportation, and communication. Mechanized farming, for example, contributed greatly to the transformation of America from a rural society to an urban society. It freed millions from food production to work in manufacturing and services. And Henry Ford's assembly line didn't just speed production. It made production more efficient (of course!) which, in turn, helped keep the price of products down. Indeed, Ford's goal was to price his automobile so the average family could afford it. And consider the impact of the automobile. Coupled with the paved highway, it contributed to the decline of business in small towns across America by making it easy to shop in larger nearby cities. And it spread families apart as each new generation, especially those in smaller communities, sought economic opportunities elsewhere. Later, networks of freeways in cities made it possible for workers to live farther from their jobs—which contributed to the development of metropolitan areas.

These examples could go on and on. The point is, technological developments that were ultimately made possible by writing resulted in fundamental changes in societies. As illustrated by today's native inhabitants of the Amazon rain forests and most Native Americans before contact with Europeans, cultural groups which have no written form of their language live very differently—virtually in the Stone Age. There is limited invention, change is slow, and tradition plays a dominant, enduring role, with tasks carried out the same way generation after generation. They are, in a sense, frozen in time. Just imagine, no telephone, no cataract surgery, no computer, no electric appliances, no antibiotics, no automobile, no airplanes, no magazines, no television, ... and a life expectancy of 35 or 40 years!

Writing and the subsequent Age of Invention even affected the existence of some cultural groups. Historically, contact between those who possessed a written form of their language and those who did not usually led to the destruction of the non-writing people or fundamental change in their culture. Aside from new diseases and the missionaries, this was brought about in two ways. First, during their quest for resources, the advanced weaponry of the writing people enabled them, when deemed necessary, to destroy or to subjugate those who were less developed. (Where are the Karankawas?) Second, the everyday conveniences possessed by the writing groups, such as the mirror, rifle, colorful clothing, and utensils, were often desired by the non-writing people. As they adopted these conveniences, they inevitably became dependent upon the more advanced group and were assimilated to some extent into the dominant writing culture. The non-writing culture, then, was fundamentally changed or just gradually disappeared. The culture of the Eskimos of the North Slope, for example, was significantly altered with the adoption of the rifle, snowmobile, conventional frame housing, and television. And while they were completely self-sufficient before, they now need many items that can only be provided by others. These processes continue today as illustrated in the rain forests of Brazil—despite the growing sensitivity to and appreciation for cultural differences.

But application of technology by a cultural group, whether constructive or destructive, is determined by its values, morality, and regard for the rights of others—concerns not addressed here. Whatever the case, the flood of scientific and technological achievements made possible by writing has forever altered the path of the great human adventure. We are now in the initial stage of extending our adventure far beyond Earth.

The Need For Writing Today

Teaching children how to write composition has been a goal in American schools since colonial times. Its designation as one of the three Rs assured its prominence in the curriculum—or so it seemed. New priorities and the crowding of the curriculum with additional subjects in the 20th century reduced the amount of time for writing instruction and diminished the effectiveness of the writing program. Fortunately, the surge of interest in writing during the 1970s and 1980s indicates a renewed commitment to teaching children how to write. This commitment is also reflected in the volume of research about writing that began to expand rapidly during the 1970s.

Why has the ability to write been so highly valued for so long? Our founding fathers recognized that in order for this grand experiment in democracy to succeed, that if we were to remain free to choose our destiny, we had to be increasingly well-informed and be able to compete effectively in world commerce. Reading and writing were judged to be indispensible to our success.

Today the ability to write is universally recognized as one of the components of literacy. One must be able to read **and** to write in order to be literate. He who is literate is better equipped to gain the knowledge and job skills requisite to "the good life." Otherwise, his career opportunities are significantly limited, even his ability to function on a daily basis in a modern society is seriously hampered. Sadly, the illiterate struggles to cope with today's complex, changing world because he is equipped to function, in a sense, in a preliterate society centuries ago.

To realize fully the importance of literacy, one need look no farther than the Third World—or, for that matter, at those in our own society who are illiterate. Without exception, the literacy rates in Third World nations are quite low—much lower than that in the industrialized, modern world. As a matter of fact, it is widely accepted that the low literacy rates are one of the primary reasons for the continuing existence of the Third World! Nations have, as a result, designated the achievement of a high level of literacy as a national goal. Otherwise, they fear that they will be unable to compete effectively in the world economy, and never have a realistic chance of achieving the high standard of living found in the modern world.

There have been predictions that computers and voice-activated word processors will somehow make writing obsolete. This is nonsense! Whether dictating to a voice-activated word processor, typing, or writing with pencil in hand, one is engaged in the act of composing. Composing is the essence of writing. (Why else would we refer to it as written composition!) Just as the musician composes to create music, the writer composes when he writes. But instead of stringing notes and relating them to lyrics, the writer strings words into sentences and weaves sentences into paragraphs to communicate ideas and to create moods, images, and feelings. Voice-activated equipment will ease the mechanics of the process, but the writer will continue to be faced with the tasks of generating ideas and constructing messages to convey his meanings to his readers. He will have to select words, compose meaningful sentences and paragraphs, and organize paragraphs into an effective sequence.

Even the video recorder will not obviate the need for writing. We've all encountered: "Put it in writing!" Writing is often required when someone wants to make a request or offer a suggestion. This policy encourages individuals to think through their ideas seriously and discourages half-baked and off-the-cuff thinking.

Writing is also used when someone wishes to maximize the impact of a communication. A written reprimand is more threatening than an oral reprimand. And we send memos and quarterly reports because we recognize that writing contains an aura of officialese and an element of permanence not present in oral communications. Writing also provides legal safeguards since it provides a tangible record of communications. A receipt or copy of a memo cannot be denied. Because of these elements, writing plays an essential role in communications in the world of business and at all levels and branches of government.

As illustrated by the following partial list, writing also plays a vital role in the everyday lives of people.

Application for health/life insurance
Registration for a class
Writing checks
Grocery list
Application for a job
Application for auto/property insurance
Application for driver's license
Things to do list
Resume
Note to a friend
Get well note
Filling out report about auto accident
Thank you note
Invitations
Note/letter of condolence
Personal letter
Business letter/memo
Letter to the editor
Vehicle registration
Taking notes at a meeting/from a printed source
Register to vote
Hotel registration
Register for a convention
Form for airline ticket
Contract to purchase/sell something
Contract for a job
Application for credit card
Reports (of all kinds)
Warranty forms
Outline material
Directions telling how to go somewhere
Directions telling how to do/make something
Research paper
Filling out renter's contract
Medical history at physician's office
Property appraisal
Classified ad
List of estate assets/liabilities

Last will and testament

Undoubtedly, there will continue to be a need to learn to write!

Aside from these practical needs for writing and the historical impact of writing, writing provides additional benefits. One is its inherent tendency to stimulate our intellect or depth of thinking. Writing is a slower, more deliberate process than speaking—which leads us to think about our subject in greater depth. It also provides a tangible record that is inevitably examined and improved. Most of us simply can't resist the temptation to tinker with our material, especially since word processors have made it so easy. Examination of our material often stimulates new ideas about our subject and expansion or refinement of those already noted. Writing, then, lends itself to more thorough consideration of a topic, a problem, or an issue. These characteristics, in turn, promote development of mental discipline, especially since writing must meet stricter standards than speech and since it requires attention to items not included in speech.

Writing also provides a means of expressing our innate creative desires. Indeed, our need to create, our need to express ourselves aesthetically, whether in music, sculpture, painting, or writing, truly sets us apart from all other life on Earth. We have, as a result, a growing collection of literary works—plays, essays, novels, short stories, poems, and such—that has been created for our enjoyment and adds meaning to our lives. Even our favorite movies and television programs are based on scripts! Our lives would certainly be less meaningful without the literary contributions of Homer, Shakespeare, Poe, Thoreau, Sinclair Lewis, Twain, Kipling, Rolvaag, Faulkner, Asimov, ...

The Current Status of Writing

The continuing need for writing and the high priority placed on writing should result in steadily improving writing skills of American children. Unfortunately, this has not necessarily been the case. Writing programs have had mixed results, often less than desired.

Students' Writing Skills

In 1984 a report on a federally financed ten-year study of children's writing skills was released by the National Assessment of Educational Progress.[1] Ninety-five thousand students from across the nation were included in the study. Writing skills of 9, 13, and 17-year-old students had been assessed in 1974, 1979, and 1984.

The study focused on three types of writing: informative, persuasive, and imaginative. Writing samples were judged on two levels: first, whether the student accomplished the task, and, second, for organization, content, grammar and usage, spelling, punctuation, and choice of words.

The study concluded that there was "a clear cause for concern about the writing proficiency of the nation's students." It reported that 62 percent of the 17-year-olds, 81 percent of the 13-year-olds, and 97 percent of the 9-year-olds wrote unsatisfactory informative prose. It also reported that 76 percent of the 17-year-olds, 83 percent of the 13-year-olds, and 95 percent of the 9-year-olds could not adequately write imaginative material. Persuasive writing skills were in even worse condition!

This study reinforced the findings of other studies. It is also supported by what experienced teachers have been saying for years—that many students' writing skills are poor. Even worse, many teachers with long service records have been complaining that students' writing skills have **deteriorated** noticeably during the last 25 years. The study also supports my observations about the writing skills of some students who enrolled in my classes in college and in public schools. It also reflects the negative attitude many students have toward writing and about themselves as writers.

Writing in the Elementary School

Writing has traditionally been assigned a rather high priority in elementary schools, beginning with its designation as one of the three Rs. In practice, however, the high priority often has not been reflected in instructional time. It has usually been included in the language arts block, along with handwriting, spelling, grammar and usage, oral expression, and listening. Reading, although a part of the language arts, is usually assigned a separate time block and taught as a subject in itself. Most of the language arts block is often consumed by direct practice on grammar and usage, punctuation, capitalization, spelling, handwriting, listening, and oral expression. This has resulted in limited time for children to spend writing—that is, thinking, writing, revising, editing, and rewriting.

Compounding this serious deficiency in instructional time is the failure to adjust the teaching loads of writing teachers so that they will have adequate at-school time to meet their disportionately heavy grading and evaluating responsiblities. While spelling tests, math tests, comprehension checks in reading, and paperwork in most other subject areas are usually easy to score and to evaluate, samples of children's writing are another matter. Depending on the type of material, grade level, and the individual child's writing problems, the time needed to evaluate and to provide feedback will usually require at least ten minutes per paper. Unfortunately, this is not usually reflected in writing teachers' loads. They are expected to teach as many classes as those teachers who are assigned to other subject areas. Writing teachers, as a result, are expected to use more of their after-school time evaluating their students' paperwork. This deficiency is caused in part, no doubt, by the failure to appreciate fully the complex nature of writing and the amount of time needed to become an effective writer.

Writing in Teacher Training Programs

College programs designed to produce elementary school teachers typically structure part of the required coursework according to the subject areas that are taught in public schools. Students are required to complete courses in the curriculum and methods of teaching science, math, social studies, reading, and language arts, with support areas in art, music, and health and physical education. As in the elementary school, reading is typically taught as a course in itself. In fact, students are usually required to complete **two** courses in reading. At one university where I was a faculty member, students majoring in elementary education were even encouraged to complete a minor (18 semester hours) in reading or listening! Writing receives no similar special distinction—despite the fact that it is an inherently more difficult task and that children's writing skills are notoriously worse than their reading abilities. Instead, it is included in the single language arts course with those other subject areas noted above. The available instructional time for preparing these students to be writing teachers is usually limited to about 8 to 12 hours, and treatment, of course, is limited in depth.

As a matter of fact, up until the mid-1970s there was usually little or no instruction about teaching writing in this language arts course. (I remember well the undergraduate language arts course that I completed in 1966—with no attention to written composition.) And this brings up an interesting point: Since the late 1960s, children's writing skills have actually deteriorated even though teachers have been receiving more instruction about teaching writing.

Recent Developments

During the 1980s some college programs focused greater attention on preparing teachers to teach writing, while little or nothing changed in others. Those institutions that sought to improve their programs usually added a course, often linking writing with reading.

Greater attention was also focused on developing children's writing skills in public schools during the 1980s—with mixed results. High priorities were placed on writing in curriculum guides, and more writing experiences were built into commercially available language arts programs. The reading specialist was expanded into a literacy specialist in some schools. In some schools "whole language" programs replaced the traditional curricular arrangement, integrating the various language arts in learning experiences that required development and application of multiple skills in context. In many elementary and junior high schools, however, reading continued to enjoy a separate instructional period while the remaining language arts were assigned another. Time for students to write continued to be limited. In addition, most writing teachers, like others, continued to be provided only one prep period each day.

Further eroding the effort to improve children's writing skills, I believe, is a growing unwillingness among teachers to use their after-school time grading papers. The failure to provide sufficient prep time for writing teachers seems, unfortunately, to have contributed to a feeling of hopelessness among some writing teachers and growing resentment as expressed by one teacher: "If the (school) district doesn't consider writing important enough to provide me with adequate time to grade papers at school, I'm not going to consider it important enough to grade papers at home." Children's writing skills suffer—and our future is diminished.

NOTES

1. Arthur N. Applebee and others, <u>Writing Trends Across the Decade, 1974-1984, Report No. ETS-15-W-01,</u> (Princeton, NJ: National Assessment of Educational Progress, 1986.) ED 273 680.

CHAPTER 2: THE NATURE OF WRITING

If we are to be effective writing teachers, we must first understand the nature of writing. Essentially, writing is the process of thinking and recording on paper, computer disk, or other medium, commonly accepted symbols that represent those thoughts for a communicative purpose. The symbols represent sounds of the spoken language and, when used in appropriate combinations, represent the words and sentence structures of that language. It is foremost a mental process, with manipulation of the writing instrument or keyboard merely serving as a means of revealing one's thoughts to others.

Although writing is based on speech, it really isn't, as the kindergarten teacher suggests, "talk written on paper." It is more accurate to describe it as *disciplined thinking* written on paper. Talk typically includes numerous meaningless utterances, unnecessary repetition, and sentence fragments. (Just listen!) Writing does not. Speech includes intonations and is often accompanied by subtle facial expressions and gestures. Writing does not. Speech is often a spontaneous event in response to a social situation—with little or no forethought. Writing is a deliberate act that requires planning and organization—and greater concentration. Oral expression that is not spontaneous, such as a speech or a report, is nearly always based on a *written* outline, notes, or a complete text.

The Difficulty of Writing

As indicated in Chapter 1, the process of writing is a more time-consuming, difficult task than speaking or reading. The writer must select the appropriate words, then construct sentences and paragraphs that represent his thoughts. But this is usually only the beginning. Unlike speaking and reading, revision plays an important role in the writing process. Most written materials are rewritten at least once—and for good reason! The original draft is available for examination and, since the writer understands the greater penalty for errors associated with writing, he cannot resist the urge to check for errors and to improve how his message is worded. The problem is, something can be said in different ways, and the writer must decide how he wants to say it. Even the professional writer may struggle with a passage for days before he is satisfied. He inserts, deletes, and rearranges words and sentences as he strives to express his meanings and to help his anticipated readers understand and create the appropriate feelings and images. Revisions continue until the writer is satisfied—or until a deadline or fatigue precludes further revision. Interestingly, no matter how many times the writer has "finished" a work, he invariably finds ways to improve it each time he examines it again. Hemingway's goal of two type-written pages per day attests to this difficult nature of writing.

Several factors contribute to this difficult nature of writing:

1. Of the four modes of communication, we have the least experience with writing. It is the least frequently used on a daily basis since language is first oral in nature. In addition, less time is usually allotted for writing instruction in schools than for reading instruction. Less experience and less instruction result in less proficiency—whatever the skill.

2. Speech appears spontaneously without any formal instruction as the child strives to satisfy his needs and wants. It is learned merely as means to an end. An infant soon begins vocalizations and differentiating sounds as a means of affecting his environment—such as getting a diaper change or getting fed. Writing, however, does not appear spontaneously. It must be taught. Becoming a writer must be a conscious goal of the learner, an end in itself. It requires a deliberate effort on the part of the learner and on the part of those who are to teach him. It normally includes specific learning experiences that are carefully designed and sequenced by persons charged with the responsibility of teaching the learner.

3. Speech occurs in a social context. During his efforts to express his meanings, the speaker is often aided by his listeners who provide immediate feedback through facial expressions, head nods, and questions or interruptive comments that help complete or clarify the speaker's intended meanings. In contrast, writing is a solitary, internal process. This requires greater self-discipline, language facility, and maturity in motivation.

4. Although writing is based on oral language, becoming a competent writer requires more time than learning to talk or learning to read. Thus, it requires greater patience and determination to sustain the necessary effort.

5. Writing is based on speech and requires the use of symbols that represent speech. This poses problems in preciseness since some meaning-bearing elements in speech, such as intonations, are difficult to represent in writing. It also implies that the process of writing is more abstract—considerably removed from the world of things, events, and sensations.

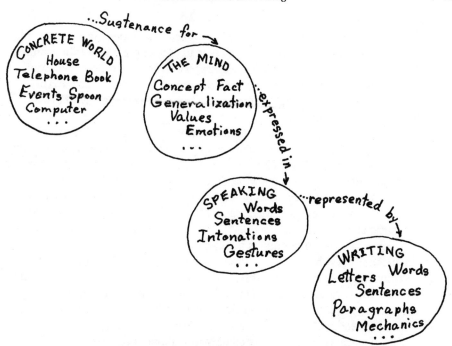

6. Unique to writing is an inherent conflict between the motor component and the mind. The mind is geared through experience to the rather fast pace of thinking associated with oral language. Words are spoken as they occur in the thinking process. But typing or manipulation of the writing instrument proceeds at a much slower pace. The writer's mind strives to speed ahead at its accustomed pace, but lagging thoughts flowing through the hand hinder its progress. Unfortunately, a word, phrase, or an idea is occasionally forgotten before the hand can act—and the hand occasionally omits a word as it hurries to keep pace with the writer's thoughts. The writer's mind is challenged, then, to maintain not only its creativity and clear flow ideas, but also to retain earlier words and sentences long enough for the hand to record them.

7. Society *expects* a higher level of preciseness and conformity to standards in writing than it requires in speech. While sentence fragments, repetitions, and meaningless utterances are common but usually overlooked or tolerated in speech, writing containing such qualities is severly criticized. For example, those who include sentence fragments, misspellings, or confusing organization in their memos and letters are commonly penalized in the business community.

8. Linguists have long recognized that *comprehension precedes production* in language development. We understand our native language before we learn to speak or to write it. Likewise, a student of a foreign language is able to understand the language when he hears it before he can speak or write it. This

occurs because listening and reading are receptive modes that require the mere decoding of symbols another person used to express ideas. In contrast, writing is an *expressive* mode that requires one to engage in the more complex process of encoding his thoughts into a message. This process requires selecting, organizing, and presenting appropriate language symbols in an understandable context.

9. Linguists have also recognized that *reception exceeds expression.* Our listening vocabulary is larger than our speaking vocabulary, and our reading vocabulary is larger than our writing vocabulary. We often grasp the general meanings of new words when we hear or read them in context, but avoid using them in our writing because of limited familiarity. The writer is not aided by a pre-existing context. He must search for words in his own vocabulary as he constructs his messages.

10. The process of writing requires attention to elements that are not included in speech, such as spelling, capitalization, and punctuation.

11. Writing requires a considerably higher level of concentration than does speech for several reasons. The writer must, as noted above, meet more stringent standards and focus on elements unique to writing. In addition, he must meet the challenge of constructing the required clear flow of ideas in his writing from his normally less organized thoughts associated with speech. He must also retain words and sentences long enough in his mind for his hand to record them.

Developmental Stages of Writing

Observations of preschool children and students up through junior high have led me to conclude that becoming a competent writer is apparently a developmental process. Recognizable stages or milestones occur during this process. They occur in the following sequence.

1. **Observation of Someone Writing**. The first important experience for the child is that he observe another person in the act of reading and, more importantly, in the act of writing. This experience is important because it causes the child to begin to understand the nature and purpose of writing. It usually occurs in the home during the preschool years.

2. **Scribble.** Scribble also usually occurs in the home during the preschool years, and it may continue into kindergarten. Scribble is important because it indicates that the child has developed the understanding that marks on paper (or other medium) represent meanings in speech, and because it allows him to practice some of the skills associated with the act of writing. The child may begin to develop basic orientations of left-to-right and top-to-bottom.

Scribble normally proceeds from a beginning stage, where no identifiable marks are included, to a final stage where some letters can be recognized. These letters are used at random. They do not conform to established letter-sound relationships. Appearance of these letters is usually the result of informal instruction by a parent or older sibling, or by the child's astute observations of older family members' writings. Scribbling resembles spontaneous play with no forethought and is usually accompanied by vocalization of the message. The child simply begins "writing" his first thought and continues what Bereiter and Scardamalia call a "what next" approach as he thinks each next statement.[1] The child will happily "read" his "story" when asked to do so.

3. **Recognizing Letters and Copying Isolated Words.** In this stage the child begins to recognize letters and copy isolated words—usually including his name, the day of the week, the name of his school, and names of items that are labeled in his classroom. The teacher initially provides models on paper for each child at his desk, then at the chalkboard. This is done because a young child has difficulty transferring visual images from a distant, verticle plane, the chalkboard, to a nearby horizontal surface, his desk. The child experiences a sense of pride when he writes **his** name and other words of special meaning.

4. **The Dictated Personal Experience Story.** In this stage writing is viewed as "talk written on paper." Children tell about a group experience, and the teacher writes what they say on a chart or chalkboard. The teacher guides the children by leading a discussion before writing and by asking leading questions during writing. Earliest stories are read aloud by the teacher, but the pupils are encouraged to read the stories as they become able. Students usually copy the story after reading it. Dictation usually proceeds from group-dictated stories about group experiences to stories of each child.

This milestone is important because it allows the child to see an accurate representation of his language on paper, and because it enables him to expand his ability to recognize letters, to begin development of a basic sight vocabulary, and to begin developing concepts such as capital letter, period, and question mark. It also reinforces earlier orientations about left-to-right and top-to-bottom. Although many concepts and skills are introduced, teachers are careful not to expect too much from their pupils. They are typically supportive, modeling desirable writing skills and techniques, and emphasizing praise rather than corrective feedback. Greater priority is placed on building children's confidence in themselves as individuals and as writers than on expecting children to master numerous mechanical skills.

5. **The Beginning Independent Writer.** In this stage the writer is venturing into his own earliest writings. It is charcterized by his enthusiasm for writing and confidence in himself as a writer—provided his teacher has presented writing as "talk on paper" and has been supportive, avoiding negative criticism. He believes that he can write anything. Writing spontaneously with little or no forethought, his stories are often fragmentary and poorly organized because he uses the "what next" approach. He often writes the

same sentence pattern repeatedly, using simple sentences and an occasional sentence fragment. Emphasis continues to be placed on expressing ideas, with attention to spelling and mechanics on an as-requested basis.

6. **The Independent Writer**. The child at this level is clearly more skilled in writing sentences and paragraphs, and more knowledgeable about spelling and mechanics. The simple sentence is not nearly so dominant in his writing; compound sentences and even some subordination are used. He proceeds from writing his own personal experience stories, to writing original stories and practical materials, such as friendly letters, notes, directions, and reports. His writing process has moved from the "what next" approach to a point where some forethought is apparent as he begins to think about his audience.

7. **The Experimental Writer**. In this stage the writer fully matures. He becomes venturesome, trying out elements, such as the metaphor or flashback, and new types of materials, such as plays. It is accompanied by a rapid growth in writing vocabulary, a wide range of reading interests, and an interest in memorizing facts. The writer begins to comprehend other points of view. His logical thinking is noticeably improved, and his arguments in editorials become much more effective. His improved abilities to handle direct discourse and manipulate sentences enable him to concentrate more on exploring and expressing ideas.

It should be noted that it is not always easy to identify clearly a writer's level of development because the end of one level closely blends into the next level. In addition, writers often continue some behaviors of the preceding level when beginning to display those of the next level.

Wide Range In Skill Development

Although children normally experience the above growth pattern, observation of their writing behaviors and examination of their materials reveal that they vary considerably in their development as writers. Each apparently develops his own style of writing, and each grows at his own rate. As a matter of fact, not all writers achieve the highest level, the experimental writer. In a typical class, then, there will be a considerable range in writing abilities. This range normally expands as children proceed through the grades. I have observed both virtual non-writers and very mature writers in college classes, and exceptional eighth grade students who wrote as well as the typical college student. Teachers obviously need to determine each child's developmental needs and be flexible in their expectations.

Types of Writing

Writers write for various purposes:
    To inform
    To inquire

To request
To respond to a request
To console or comfort
To entertain others
To entertain themselves
To explore their own ideas
To satisfy a need for achievement
To question
To persuade

Materials range from personal letters and diaries, on the one hand, to reports, editorials, and appraisals on the other. A comprehensive list of the different types of materials commonly included in the school curriculum is presented in Chapter 6.

Regardless of the type of material, there are four basic rhetorical modes used in writing. They include *description, narration, exposition*, and *persuasion*. They are hierarchial in nature, with each successive level adding an element or elements to that of the preceding level.

Description is the most basic mode. It is used in many types of materials. A description consists of statements about the attributes of whatever is being described. References to appearance (size, shape, and color), taste, smell, sound, and how something feels are commonly included. There is no reference to time or sequence, but merely impressions of that being described. References to relative location of parts are included as appropriate. Describing activities are rather common in elementary schools, sometimes in the form of sentence expansion exercises and picture or object descriptions.

The *narrative mode* adds the elements of time and sequence. Processes and directions are described in the order in which they should be carried out, and events are usually described in chronological order. Examples of narrative writing in the elementary school are the personal experience story, the original story, and directions telling how to do something or make something.

Expository writing attempts to explain relationships. Attention is focused on *how* and *why* questions. It not only includes descriptions and sequencing of events, but also provides explanations about cause-and-effect relationships between events, or significance of parts to each other. Explanations about the effects of brushing our teeth regularly, or why it sleets rather than hails are examples of expository writing.

Persuasive writing adds the elements of judgment and advice or recommendation. It explains the goodness or worth of an idea, action, or thing, and it attempts to influence the reader's attitudes or actions by providing supportive explanations. The argument, whether for or against something, typically includes a position statement and reasons that support the position. It may include quotes from respected individuals, facts, and analogies to strengthen the argument. A description of something or a summary of past events also may be included. A letter to the editor or an editorial in the school paper about the dress code might be appropriate for upper grade children.

Whether writing a friendly letter, a personal experience story, or a research report, one or more of these modes are usually apparent. Many materials, then, will include use of more than one mode. For example, a writer will usually describe something when telling about some event in a letter or story. An editorial against smoking might include explanations about why people decide to smoke, a description of the appearance of a smoker's lungs, stages of smoking, how smoking specifically affects one's health, and a recommendation that smokers quit smoking.

Implications

What does all this suggest for teaching children to write? Some of the more apparent implications are:

1. Considerably more instructional time and writing experiences should be provided in most schools.
2. Since writing is based on speech, effective speaking abilities are an asset to development of effective writing skills.
3. Established speech patterns and usages will be reflected in writing. Instruction, then, should also focus on the appropriateness of those items in writing.
4. Parents should be supportive of their preschool children's scribble by providing needed materials and responding to it in a positive manner.
5. Parents should read and write in the presence of their preschool children on a regular basis.
6. Since children develop as writers in a usual pattern, writing experiences can be sequenced accordingly.
7. Since children develop as writers at different rates, teachers need to be flexible in their expectations.
8. Early writing instruction can be effectively integrated with early reading instruction through the dictated group-experience story.
9. Writing instruction should stress the primary mental aspects of writing— selecting and organizing words into sentences, arranging sentences in the best sequence, and arranging paragraphs in the best sequence.
10. Since a writer's thoughts about a subject mature as he writes and revises his material, his final draft will usually differ somewhat from his initial draft.
11. Since writing is ultimately a solitary process, a variety of writing aids, such as the dictionary, should be readily available.
12. Since writing must meet stricter standards than speech, the writing process should include time for the writer to think about his subject before he begins writing, and time to re-examine his writing and rewrite it as needed.
13. Since the hand must forever hurry as it strives to keep pace with the mind, expectations about handwriting neatness, spelling, and other surface features in initial outlines and working drafts should emphasize legibility, not exceptional neatness, and expression of ideas, not preciseness and correctness in mechanical details.

14. Since writing requires a high level of concentration, a reasonably quiet writing environment is conducive to effective writing.
15. Since clarity of purpose is reflected in clarity of writing, the teacher should emphasize purpose of a material before and during writing.
16. Direct practice on descriptive, narrative, expository, and persuasive writing should be introduced in that order.
17. Children's writing skills normally lag behind their reading skills because writing is an inherently more complex task.
18. If the writing competence of American youth continues to deteriorate, our standard of living will decline.

NOTES

1. Carl Bereiter and Marlene Scardamalia, "From Conversation to Composition: The Role of Instruction in a Developmental Process," <u>Advances In Instructional Psychology</u>, Vol. 2; (Hillsdale, NJ: Lawrence Erlbaum Associates, Publishers, 1982).

CHAPTER 3: DEFINING PROGRAM EFFECTIVENESS

Teacher conversations at the end of the school day sometimes focus on anxieties about lack of pupil achievement or lack of pupil interest in required learning activities. During one of these conversations with a colleague, she said that when she announced a writing activity earlier that day, some of her sixth graders responded with the following usual comments:

"Do we have to?"

"Let's do something else!"

"How long does it have to be?"

"Is it gonna be for a grade?"

Then she looked at the pile of papers on her desk and asked, "When am I ever going to get these papers graded?" She began flipping through the stack of papers, then stopped and said, "And just look at this! Is this kid *ever* going to remember the difference between *then* and *than*?

Pupil feedback and teacher anxieties like those expressed above are not uncommon—especially when the subject is writing. When a writing activity is announced to a group of sixth graders or, for that matter, to a group of freshmen, some pupils respond unfavorably. Many older children simply do not like to write. Like many adults, they lack confidence in their writing abilities and resist writing—even avoid it when possible.

Children don't bring this attitude to school when they enter kindergarten. Consider the four-year-old's joy in scribbling and her eagerness to share it. Ask her to read what she has written and she will "read" at length with obvious satisfaction. This attitude is also rather common among kindergarten and first grade children. They are excited about group experiences and the stories their teachers write on the chalkboard as they tell about those experiences, and they are eager to write their own stories. They *believe* they can write.

Middle school children who continue to have confidence in their writing abilities also often respond favorably to opportunities to write and look forward to sharing what they have written. Like some adults, they actually *enjoy* writing even though they realize that writing is a time-consuming task that requires considerable effort. Unfortunately, these students tend to be the exception in many classrooms.

What causes many children to develop a negative attitude toward writing? What classroom strategies and practices promote development of positive attitudes toward writing and most effectively help children learn to write? This chapter reponds to these questions through a careful examination of each of the following:

1. Children's Misconceptions About Writing
2. Adults' Criticisms of Their Writing Experiences in School
3. Children's Acquisition of Speech
4. Research and the Author's Observations About Effective Writing Strategies and Practices

Comparative studies that examined the relative effectiveness of two or more strategies or practices are included in this chapter. Selected studies that focused on only one effective strategy or technique and practices that I observed to be effective while teaching children to write are also included.

The Negative Attitude Toward Writing

Teachers are all too aware of the negative attitude many children have about writing. They also realize that this unfavorable attitude often impedes development of effective writing skills and have, as a result, focused considerable effort on determining the causes of this attitude problem. Part of the problem undoubtedly can be attributed to the nature of writing itself—as described in Chapter 2. Writing is a time-consuming task that requires more concentration and effort than speaking or reading. And sooner or later, writers learn that writing *must* conform to stricter standards than speech—and that to violate these standards usually carries a greater penalty.

Part of the attitude problem also can probably be attributed to misconceptions about writing that some children develop. Some misconceptions that I have observed are:

1. **Writing is mere talk written on paper.** While this belief is properly promoted with kindergarteners and first graders as a means of developing their confidence, it can be a source of discouragement to a child later when he realizes that written sentences must be "complete" and must be correctly punctuated, and that words must be correctly spelled and capitalized.
2. **One just begins writing when he needs to write something.** Yet teachers often insist on outlining and other prewriting activities.
3. **Adults never have to rewrite; they write perfectly on first effort.**
   The child simply doesn't realize, for example, the struggle the author of one of his favorite stories went through when writing it. His natural confidence

and trust in the abilities of adults leads him to a false conclusion about the act of writing. He becomes discouraged when he compares his inability to produce a perfectly written paper on first effort. He does not realize that writing is a **process** that normally necessitates more than one draft.

4. **Rewriting merely requires one to check for spelling and to recopy material neatly.** This results in no change in **what** is said or **how** it is said. Yet, teachers often urge changes in how the message is written.

5. **A writing task isn't important unless it's for a grade.** The child fails to appreciate writing as a useful means of communication or entertainment. It's just something that has to be done in school.

These misconceptions provide some direction about how to teach children to write. First, even though significant differences exist between writing and talking, I believe teachers are correct in encouraging young beginning writers to believe that writing is talk written on paper. This is a natural extension of children's language familiarity. Teachers need not be alarmed by the frequency of errors in young writers' early efforts. But instead of concentrating on correction of their errors, the teacher should stress praise and enjoyment of writing. This will build children's confidence in themselves as individuals and as writers. As children mature as writers, development of a sense of audience will help them more fully recognize and accept the differences between talking and writing, and appreciate the importance of writing correctly.

Second, even the earliest narrative writing experience, the group-dictated personal experience story, should be preceded by a teacher-led discussion about the experience and accompanied by questions during writing. These discussions and questions will help children begin to develop a sense of organization.

These misconceptions also suggest that teachers should provide examples that illustrate how important planning and rewriting are to adults. Visits to the local newspaper, seeing the teacher as a writer engaged in the writing process, and use of commercially-available materials that describe, for example, how a children's book is produced, all can help children realize that writing is a challenging process for adults. The filmstrip/tape, "How a Picture Book is Made: The Island of the Skog," is an excellent example.[1]

These misconceptions further indicate that measures need to be taken to help children value writing in itself—not just as a means to a grade. Focusing writing on their experiences, interests, and needs can, like children's literature, help children appreciate writing. They need to remember that every favorite story had to be written.

Finally, these misconceptions indicate that teachers need to emphasize expression of ideas and writing for enjoyment. Spelling and mechanics need to be de-emphasized, especially in the rough draft, and not everything should be graded.

Teaching upper-division college classes over a period of years also provided me with opportunities to gain insight into the causes of this attitude problem. I asked each of my students to make a list of experiences in school that made her "dislike" writing. The following comments are a composite of those provided by the students.

"In fourth grade, whenever we misbehaved we had to write a letter of apology to the teacher. I hated it."

"I had to write book reports on all the books I read."

"The teacher didn't take time to read carefully what I had prepared."

"My work was compared with other students' papers in class."

"I was forced to write on the spur of the moment without sufficient time to gather ideas."

"Too much pressure because of strict grading."

"The teacher graded it down because she disagreed with my opinon about what I had written."

"I was forced to read private thoughts I had written."

"We **had** to write poems and I always hated poetry."

"Teachers placed so much emphasis on mechanics. I worried more about that than what I had to say."

"Teachers would assign a certain number of words or pages."

"The teacher dissected my writing as a class project and everybody knew it was my paper."

"The teacher didn't allow us to choose the topic."

"My second grade teacher passed out a blank piece of paper during the creative writing period. She told us to write a story. That's it! I used to sit and cry—killed my creativeness for life."

"Once in a while I would get a story started but time was up before the story was finished."

"No comments accompanying a bad grade."

"The teacher took the whole semester to grade my paper."

"Only the good students got to read their paper in class."

"The teacher did not believe a poem I wrote was mine, accused me of plagerizing."

"I had written a paper on something very old and dear to me. I spent a lot of time and money on this project as I wrote about my uncle's farm and house in Missouri that his grandmother built 100 years ago. The whole family was born and raised there. I obtained pictures and the building plans, etc. When I got the paper back, there were sarcastic comments where I had expressed sentimental feelings and I was angry."

It would be unfair to judge all writing teachers on the basis of the above comments. Also, the full context of each of the comments is not known. Bear in mind, however, that these comments reveal memories and feelings about experiences that have endured the test of time—they occurred from four to ten years earlier in these students' lives.

Taken at face value, the comments do provide some clues as to the causes of the negative attitude toward writing. Some of the comments indicate actions by teachers that might be attributed to overworked teachers—too little time, or lack of teacher sensitivity to students' feelings. Some comments could be attributed to a lack of teacher understanding about the nature of writing and the writing process. One comment indicated a misplaced emphasis on surface features (mechanics), while another indicated too much emphasis on grades. Another suggested insufficient class time for writing tasks. One common comment focused on "no comments accompanying a bad grade." Ouch!

When these same students were asked about "enjoyable" writing experiences, they provided the following:

"In high school the teacher had a poem I wrote printed in the school paper."

"Sharing my stories with the class and the class liking them."

"Teachers allowed for choice and creativity in topics."

"Stories and poems were displayed in class."

"We had a creative writing club."

"I wrote a story in the second grade and my mom loved it. She still has it."

"Being able to write about silly things such as 'Have You Ever Seen A Purple Turtle?'"

"We were allowed to write letters to friends, grandparents, etc. as an assignment."

"The teacher told me I was creative and had a great imagination."

"She used visual aids to stimulate us before we wrote."

These comments about enjoyable experiences also provide direction for helping children develop positive attitudes toward writing. They suggest that students should be given considerable freedom in choosing topics and determining lengths of materials. They also suggest that students should be given ample time to prepare for writing and enough time to finish what is started. They further suggest that teachers should respect students' opinions and feelings when expressed in writing. They imply that teachers should take time to carefully and thoughtfully respond to each child's writings, but they should not grade every paper. Teacher feedback should be reasonably prompt. They suggest that teachers should encourage students to share their written materials, but not be required to do so—especially private thoughts. They also suggest that teachers should appreciate students' ideas rather than concentrate mainly on mechanics. They indicate that display of children's writings in the classroom and publication of them in the school newspaper build student esteem and enjoyment of writing. They also reveal that a writing club and awards for writing contribute to a positive attitude toward writing. Finally, teacher compliments for good writing are appreciated—while using writing for punishment is counterproductive.

Children's Acquisition of Speech

An examination of children's acquisition of speech also provides some useful insights when formulating a strategy for teaching writing.   At birth, an infant is surrounded by a maze of sounds, images, and other sensations. Nothing has meaning. But almost immediately, he is able to differentiate vocalizations to communicate his various discomforts to others. Mothers learn quickly to distinguish an "I'm hungry" cry from an "I want to be held" cry.

The first words appear at about one year of age, and, by his fifth year, he has developed considerable facility with the basic syntax of his native language—whether it is English, Spanish, Russian, or Arabic. This has been accomplished without the benefit of any formal lessons about verbs or teachers who helped him analyze his language. He has learned to talk by using language rather than by critically analyzing its structure. He listened, tried it out, made needed adjustments, and tried again—until his vocalizations resulted in the desired responses. Speech, then, was learned implicitly. It was not a conscious goal, but merely a means to an end. It was learned in an environment where models were available, where others responded to his meanings rather than his language forms, where his real concerns were focal points, and where his efforts to talk were prized by others.

The process of acquiring speech suggests that writing experiences should focus on *real* experiences of children. It implies that the teacher should be a writer, and that teachers should praise children's writing efforts—with a minimum of critical feedback. It suggests that teachers should emphasize content rather than form when responding to children's writing—especially with young writers. It also implies that the study of traditional grammar is not necessary, and that mechanics should be studied only in context.

Research and Observations About Effective Strategies and Practices

Even though the above suggestions and implications do provide some direction about how to teach children to write, the gravity of the need for greater effectiveness in writing programs demands an examination of pertinent research and my observations as a professional educator. Those factors that have demonstrated a significant, positive impact on the effectiveness of writing programs are addressed in the remainder of this chapter.

The Nature of Learning to Write

It must be accepted that becoming an effective writer is a complex process that requires considerable time. Although children are usually introduced to writing in kindergarten, they cannot be expected to be reasonably skilled writers for several years. Some types of writing, such as editorials, often are not even formally introduced until the sixth or seventh grade.

Becoming an effective writer apparently is, as pointed out in Chapter 2, a developmental process. Children normally progress through recognizable stages or achieve milestones during this process. They will, however, vary somewhat in terms of the rate of development. In the typical fifth grade class, for example, there will be a considerable range of writing abilities.

What are the implications for teachers? Teaching children to write requires considerable patience and persistent determination of the teacher and the learner. Also, the teacher needs to be flexible in her expectations. She should first identify each child's developmental needs as a writer, then provide challenging, but not frustrating, learning tasks.

How does a teacher identify a child's developmental level as a writer? First, by comparing the child's writing skills with those stages described in Chapter 2. Additional clues can be gleaned from an examination of the writer's revising strategies—described later, and from a comparison with skills introduced in the curriculum at various grade levels.

Value of Writing

Examination of effective writing programs reveals that good writing tends to develop in classrooms and schools where it is valued. A high priority on writing is reflected in the serious commitment of various resources, including personnel, time, materials and equipment, curriculum, and effective activities. It is communicated to pupils by the teacher's writings and enthusiasm, by the time allotted to writing and sharing, and by space and equipment provided for a writing center and for display of children's writings. A class or school newspaper, a writing club, word processors and printers, and awards for writing achievement also communicate that writing is respected and appreciated. Teacher loads are adjusted so that writing teachers have adequate prep time to complete most of their evaluations of pupil papers at school.

Modes of Instruction

Hillocks identified four basic "modes of instruction" or basic strategies that have been employed in schools. Each is unique in terms of the role played by the teacher, the content and type of activities, and specificity and clearness of objectives to learners. He referred to them as the **presentation mode,** the **natural process mode,** the **environmental mode,** and the **individualized mode.**[2]

The **presentation mode** is characterized by what many consider to be a more structured, traditional approach to teaching. Objectives are clearly specified, and the teacher plays a high profile role, providing leadership through lectures, teacher-led discussions, and use of models to point out desired characteristics in writing. Students are given specific assignments and are expected to produce written materials that conform to teacher-provided standards and models. The teacher provides feedback to each child about his writing after he has "finished" his work.

The **natural process mode** is very loosely structured. It is student-centered, with considerable interaction among students and freedom for each student to write about whatever he wishes. Students assist each other by generating criteria and providing feedback whenever one rewrites his material. The teacher is seen as an assistant or facilitator who provides feedback and assistance, usually upon request. Formal study of models and criteria is usually avoided.

The **environmental mode** is more structured than the natural process mode, but less teacher-centered than the presentation mode. Like the presentation mode, objectives are clearly specified, and students are expected to engage in planning activities. But teacher lecture and teacher-led discussions are de-emphasized, while activities that facilitate problem solving through student interaction are stressed. Typically, before each student writes, a problem is introduced by the teacher. Criteria are also provided. The teacher may lead a brief discussion about a sample and help students apply the criteria to it. The student then interacts with a group of his peers in the problem-solving task. The interaction serves as a springboard to the individual writing. It enables the students to develop a skill(s) that they will later apply individually in a writing task. Suppose, for example, students are given the assignment of writing directions for getting from one place to another. Before writing, the students examine sample directions and discuss their adequacy according to the provided criteria. They may also practice giving directions and discuss their adequacy. Each student then applies those skills and criteria to his own efforts to write directions.

The **individualized mode** focuses on helping students on an individual basis. Each student is instructed through tutorials or programmed materials and progresses at his own rate. Teacher lectures, teacher-led activities for groups of students, and student interaction are not included.

Hillocks located those studies that focused on the effectiveness of these modes of instruction. He then clustered the studies according to mode so that he could determine the relative effectiveness of each mode. He reported that the **environmental mode** was much more effective than the other modes of instruction. Somewhat less effective were the **natural process** and **individualized modes.** Clearly least effective was the **presentation mode.**

Foci of Instruction

Hillocks also investigated the effectiveness of various activities and contents as revealed in previous studies. The study of **grammar and mechanics, sentence combining,** the **use of models,** the **use of scales, "free writing,"** and **inquiry** were examined.[3]

Grammar and mechanics included traditional concerns—study of the parts of speech, usage, and punctuation. Capitalization, handwriting, and spelling were also studied.

Sentence combining typically provides students with opportunities to practice combining short sentences into longer and more complex sentences. For example, students may practice combining ideas by combining simple sentences into compound sentences and complex sentences. This might be achieved through the use of compound subjects and predicates, appositives, and dependent clauses.

Use of models provides students with opportunities to examine examples, then apply what they have learned in their own writing. Although models of excellence are emphasized, models that contain errors are also occasionally examined.

Use of scales typically provides students with opportunities to evaluate or rate sample compositions and their own compositions according to provided criteria. These criteria may be in different forms, such as questions or scales. Questions help the students find problems in the sample material and generate ways of correcting them. The teacher typically introduces the scale and demonstrates how to use it, then leads the students in a discussion. Students then examine and discuss the adequacy of other compositions according to the criteria. This practice supposedly enables students to be more aware of the desirable qualities in a given type of material, and enhances their ability to produce that type of material.

Free writing consists of allowing students to write about whatever they wish—whether in journals or other forms that may be shared later. Such writing is usually not graded and not an integral part of the instructional program in writing, but, rather, an addendum. It is generally assumed that such writing will improve the student's "fluency."

Inquiry requires the teacher to act as a facilitator rather than as a presenter. It focuses on development of specific strategies rather than models or teacher-provided criteria. It typically focuses on some element of a type of written material, and provides students with opportunities to develop related skills. Students then apply these skills with others as they attempt to write the material. For example, a group of students is given a picture of a pathway through a forest. They are told to write a description of the scene so another group, when presented with the picture and another that presents a similar scene, can identify which is described. As groups practice identifying pictures from written descriptions, they discover how to describe visual scenes, including elements, their relative locations, sizes, shapes, and colors. A variation of this might require students to focus only on sounds that might be heard in the scene. Individual students are then expected to be more explicit when describing visual scenes in their writing, such as personal experience stories or creative stories.

Results of the studies that focused on the above activities were clustered according to each activity. The effectiveness of each was then compared with the other activities. **Inquiry** was clearly revealed to be the most effective. **Sentence combining** and **use of scales** were next in effectiveness, with nearly identical mean effects. **Use of models** was somewhat less effective, and free writing was found to be slightly less effective than **use of models**. **Study of grammar and mechanics** was revealed to be clearly least effective—possibly even detrimental to development of writing skills. This finding regarding the study of grammar deserves special attention.

It has long been recognized that in order to communicate effectively, one must be able to produce language according to the commonly accepted patterns in phonetics, morphology, and syntax. Early educators assumed that studying grammar was crucial to learning to write and, consequently, included it in the curriculum. Traditionally, children spent much time studying the rules of grammar, analyzing and diagramming sentences, and learning the terminology of language study. But this left only limited time for children to engage in the act of writing. When they did write, it was often viewed as an opportunity to check their use of grammar and mechanics more than an opportunity to express meanings for the purpose of communication.

Beginning with the Hoyt study in 1906, research began to reveal that the traditional study of grammar had little or no impact on children's ability to write.[4] Hoyt's conclusion has been reaffirmed consistently. Research by O'Hare indicated that students' syntactic maturity in writing—the length and complexity of sentence structures—was enhanced much more when students practiced combining sentences in practice materials.[5] Calkins reported that children learned punctuation skills more thoroughly when learning experiences stressed writing rather than study of punctuation in isolated sentences.[6]

In view of this research and the fact that children develop a basic understanding of the grammar of their language when learning to speak, the writing program obviously should stress writing. Study of grammar should clearly be minimized. This is supported by the fact that while grammarians understand grammar well, they are not always effective writers. And effective writers are not always well versed in the formal grammar of their language. They may not be able to tell, for example, what a predicate nominative is or give an example of a present progressive verb. The point is, a writer needs to understand and skillfully use the syntax of his language, but he does not **have** to be an expert in the formal rules and terminology of its grammar.

Usage in the Writing Program

Teaching children standard usage has been a traditional goal in English programs. Considerable time is usually spent on this task so that children will habituate standard usages in their speech and in their writing. A more realistic goal, however, is to supplement, not supplant a child's native language patterns. He is then able to function appropriately in different situations—and avoid the embarrassment and penalty associated with misuse.

Although study of usage is *not* writing, usage is an element of writing that can have considerable impact on the reader's opinion of the writer. Nonstandard usages needing most attention in my students' writing included:

Then for **than**:	I like her more **then** I like him.
Your for **you're**:	He said that **your** going also.
Was for **were**:	They **was** late for school.
Were for **where**:	He asked **were** I was going.
Their for **they're**:	**Their** going home.
Their for **there**:	Your book is over **their.**
No for **know**:	I **no** who your best friend is.
To for **too**:	I like her **to.**
To for **two**:	I ate **to** sandwiches.
Of for **have**:	You should **of** gone home.
Him for **he**:	Me and **him** went fishing.
Me for **I**:	**Me** and him went fishing.
Her for **she**:	Mary and **her** are my best friends.
Were for **we're**:	**Were** going home tomorrow.
Lets for **let's**:	**Lets** play a trick on him.

Or for **our:**   That's **or** house.
Seen for **saw:**   I **seen** him do it.
Done for **did:**   She **done** it.
By for **buy:**   I'm going to **by** some new shoes.
Close for **clothes:**   I got some new **close.**
Herd for **heard:**   I **herd** a scary sound.
Ran for **run:**   He has already **ran** home.
Don't for **doesn't:**   He **don't** like me.
Went for **gone:**   He has **went** fishing.
Come for **came:**   He **come** to school late.
Brung for **brought:**   She **brung** her lunch.
Redundant pronoun: My mom **she** is a good cook.

In response to these frequently occurring nonstandard usages, I grouped the words according to common incorrect associations and periodically reviewed each group with my students. These groups of words were then placed on the bulletin board for reference. After we had studied all of the groups of words individually, I provided my students with the following handout for reference.

Confusing Words Unconfused

1. **They're:** contraction for they are; used when a plural subject is being described.
   Example: **They're** going to the park.

   Their: a pronoun that refers to two or more people and indicates that they own or possess something.
   Example: **Their** house is on Elm street.

   There: refers to a place.
   Example: It's over **there.**

2. **Then:** refers to a sequence of events; one thing happening after something else happened.
   Example: He went to the store, **then** he went home.

   Than: refers to a preference or comparison of things or people.
   Example: He likes chocolate more **than** vanilla.
                He can run faster **than** Fred.

3. **Were:** past tense of **are**; used with a singular subject or plural subject.
   Example: If I **were** you, I'd buy that bicycle.
                Were you the one who did it?
                They **were** going fishing.

continued on next page

Where: refers to a place.
Example: **Where** are you going?

4. **Your:**   indicates someone owns something or is related.
Example: Is she **your** aunt?

You're: contraction for **you are**.
Example: **You're** going to the party, aren't you?

5. **To:**   used when telling **in the direction of, as far as,** or **attaching something**.
Example: He turned **to** the left.
The tree fell **to** the ground.
She nailed it **to** the door.

Too: means **more than enough, in addition** or **also,** or **very**.
Example: That's **too** big.
He went to the movies **too**.
He wasn't **too** happy with his new bicycle.

Two: a number.
Example: She has **two** cats.

6. **Know:**   refers to awareness of something or someone.
Example: I **know** the answer.

No: not so; opposite of yes.
Example: **No**, you cannot go to the movie.

Now: refers to the present time.
Example: **Now** is a good time to buy a house.

7. **It's:**   contraction for **it is**.
Example: **It's** getting late.

Its: shows something belongs to **it**.
Example: I stepped on **its** tail.

8. **Heard:**   awareness of a sound; past tense of **hear**.
Example: She **heard** a weird sound in the basement.

Herd: a group of animals.
Example: He sold his **herd** of cows.

9. **By:**   refers to a place or time.
Example: She stood **by** the door.

continued on next page

Buy: to purchase something.
Example: I **buy** a gallon of milk each week.

Bye: gesture or word that tells someone is leaving.
Example: She said, "**Bye**," then left.
He waved **good-bye**.

10. **Lose:**   to misplace something, experience a loss.
Example: Did you **lose** your key?

    Loose: refers to something not tight or not fastened.
Example: His tooth is **loose**.
My shoe feels **loose**

11. **Our:**   tells something belongs to two or more people, including the person talking or writing about it.
Example: That is **our** house.

    Hour: a unit of time (60 minutes).
Example: They have been swimming about an **hour**.

12. **Went:**   past tense of **go**.
Example: She **went** fishing yesterday.

    Gone: form of **go** that is always used with one or more helping words such as *have, had, has, is, are, was,* or *were.*
Example: He **was gone** by the time I arrived.
She **could have gone** but didn't want to.

13. **Run:**   to rapidly move afoot.
Example: I **run** to school every day.
I **have run** home from school each day.

    Ran: past tense of **run**.
Example: She **ran** home after school yesterday.

14. **Did:**   past tense of **do**.
Example: He **did** it yesterday.

    Done: form of **do** that is always used with one or more helping words such as *have, had,* or *are.*
Example: She **has done** that before.
The biscuits **are done**.

15. **Doesn't:**   contraction for **does not**; used with a singular subject.
Example: He **doesn't** live there.

continued on next page

Don't: contraction for **do not**; used with a plural subject.
Example: They **don't** know how to swim.

16. **He/She/I:** used as the subject of a sentence.
Example: **She** likes to ride horses.
My dad and **I** go fishing on weekends.

Him/Her/ used when something is being done to that person, or
Me: when that person is receiving something.
Example: They gave **her** an award.
They looked at Bill and **me**.

17. **Have:**   shows ownership, something that must be done, or a
helping word.
Example: I **have** two dogs.
I **have** to go home.
They **should have** gone home.

18. **Hole:**   a cavity or sharp depression in something.
Example: Sergio fell when he stepped into the **hole.**

Whole: all of something (object or group).
Example: The **whole** group showed up for cake.
He spent the **whole** summer at camp.

19. **Goes:**   present tense of **go**; indicates someone or something is
moving.
Example: Mom **goes** to the grocery store on Fridays.

Said: past tense of **say**; used to introduce a quote.
Example: Dad **said** that he was going fishing.
Dad **said**, "I'm going fishing."

20. **Close:**   nearby; the act of shutting something.
Example: Travis stood **close** to the door.
Will you please **close** the door?

Clothes: apparel, garments to be worn.
Example: I'm going to buy some new **clothes.**

21. **See:**   to observe something; used in the present tense or
future tense.
Example: I **see** a duck on the pond.
I **will see** you next summer.

Seen: form of see always used with one or more helping words.
Example: I **have seen** that movie before.

continued on next page

She **would have seen** the eclipse if she hadn't gone to sleep.

22. **Were:**   a form of the verb **be.**
              Example: They said that they **were** going.

    We're: contraction for **we are.**
              Example: **We're** going to Mexico this summer.

Some nonstandard usages, however, should probably be considered acceptable because of their widespread use. They are:
I'm going to **lay** down.
He **laid** down and took a nap.
Who did you send to the library?
It is **me/him/her.**
Everybody/everyone said that **they** ....
You can invite **whoever** you wish.
Will you **loan** me a pencil?
They divided the candy **between** the three of them.
No distinction between **shall** and **will.**

Teaching Mechanics

One issue has focused on whether to teach mechanics in isolation or in the context of children's writing. Some commercially-available English programs include considerable isolated practice on usage, capitalization, and punctuation. Textbooks and workbooks of these programs contain practice that requires students to choose, select, or insert appropriate items. Traditionally, it was widely accepted that isolated practice on mechanics was an effective way of teaching children mechanical skills in writing. Some research raises a question about this practice.

Calkins compared the effectiveness of teaching third-grade children punctuation skills in a "writing" class with the effectiveness of a "mechanics" class.[7] In the writing class children were taught punctuation skills as needs arose during writing activities. For example, quotation marks were introduced when the children wanted the characters in their stories to begin talking. Children in the mechanics class were taught punctuation marks according to the rules of usage or definition, and followed a predetemined sequence of lessons that consisted of drills and workbook exercises.

Upon completion of the learning experiences, the children in both groups were asked to describe as many different punctuation marks as they could, and writing samples of those in the writing class were examined to determine to what extent the children's use of different punctuation marks had expanded. Data revealed that children in the writing class were able to describe correctly many more different types of punctuation marks. There also was a clear difference in the depth of understanding between the two groups. Those in the writing class provided operational definitions, while those in the mechanics class tried to remember the rules they had been taught. Examination of the writing samples produced by the children in the writing group revealed that they had expanded their use of punctuation marks considerably. At the beginning of the study in September, they had used an average of 1.25 different kinds of marks. At the end of the study in February, these children were using an average of 5.62 different kinds of marks.

My work with children supports these findings. Providing children with corrective feedback in their own writing seems to enable them to understand better and to remember longer. Isolated practice may not be as effective because children do not have the personal investment in it.

Dealing With Persistent Errors

There does appear to be a place for some direct or isolated practice on mechanical skills and other skills—persistent errors. Persistent errors were, as a matter of fact, one of the more challenging tasks that I encountered as a seventh grade language arts teacher. Some children, especially those who were poor writers, simply didn't remember or seem to care to remember previous corrections when revising and writing final drafts—and continued to repeat them, sometimes even inserting new errors. How did I eventually deal with this problem? Partly through isolated practice found in the textbook and workbook. Such practice may be of value if it is used in the following manner.

After identifying a given problem, the teacher leads a student or group of students in a discussion about sample materials that illustrate correct use of that skill. This is followed by group practice with material presented via the overhead projector, then individual practice. For example, suppose students are continuing to write run-on sentences. This problem often results from the inability of students to relate punctuation marks to voice intonations, or from student attempts to combine ideas before they can write simple sentences. Using the overhead, I showed them two versions of a paragraph, one well written with simple sentences, and the other composed largely of run-on sentences. I read each paragraph aloud exactly as it was written. Students then were asked to decide which "sounded better." During the discussion, I carefully pointed out how sounds of the voice could help identify where to place periods. I then checked what they had learned by presenting another run-on paragraph and letting them decide as a group where to place the periods. Individual practice then followed.

"Sentence lifting," "paragraph lifting," and "essay lifting" also seemed to be effective ways of dealing with persistent errors. For example, I "lifted" sentences from their papers that contained a certain type of common error and put them on transparencies. We then corrected them in class. I seldom needed to provide input because some student nearly always supplied the appropriate correction.

It should be noted that the above processes are based on the principle that children learn by example, not by definition. Examples enable children to understand—just as they did when they were acquiring language. Definitions are often memorized without understanding, or memorized and then forgotten.

Writing Stimuli

There have been numerous publications comprised of writing prompts—ranging from abstract pictures without any accompanying directions to pictures with accompanying elaborate descriptions and specific purposes, and memorbilia such as an old shoe or baseball. Visits to classrooms quickly reveal the popularity of such materials with many writing teachers. Obviously, many teachers believe that getting children interested in writing is a problem and that such materials help stimulate their writing. My work with children clearly supports this belief. Which kind of stimuli is most effective?

Golub and Frederick examined the effects of different types of pictures on the writing of fourth and sixth grade children.[8] Concrete pictures and abstract pictures, some in color and some black and white, were used as stimuli. Sixty-three linguistic varibles were examined in the children's compositions. No significant differences were found among the different variables—regardless of the type of picture.

Brossell investigated how different amounts of detail in the stimulus affected the writing of college seniors.[9] Stimuli ranged from the lowest, which consisted of a brief phrase and a vague purpose, to the elaborate, which consisted of a paragraph that included a description of a fictitious event and a rather clear purpose. He found no significant differences in their writing, regardless of the amount of detail and clarity of purpose in the stimuli.

Apparently, the amount of detail is not a significant factor. I believe, however, that a *variety* of types of stimuli does make a difference, as does a child's freedom to choose from three or four stimuli rather than be given one stimulus and told to base his writing on it. A variety of stimuli and writing activities that my students responded to quite favorably is presented in Chapter 5.

Prewriting Discussion

Some studies have focused on the effectiveness of prewriting discussion. Beeker's study is representative.[10] Fifth graders were asked to write about three films. Children in one group simply began writing after viewing a film. Those in another group participated in a large-group discussion after viewing the film, then began writing. Children in the third group participated in paired discussions after viewing the film, then wrote. Examination of the children's compositions revealed that children who participated in no discussion wrote the fewest T-units. Those who participated in paired discussions wrote the most T-units. These findings seem logical and are consistent with those of similar studies. Prewriting discussion clearly results in more writing.

Outlining Before Writing

Many teachers require their pupils to outline their ideas in some fashion before they begin writing. These teachers argue that outlining provides time for the pupil to think—time for him to generate ideas and organize them in a more effective sequence. Research supports this practice. Stallard examined the writing behavior of "good student writers" and compared their behavior with that of randomly selected writers.[11] "Good writers" were found to spend much more time in prewriting than other students, 4.18 minutes versus 1.2 minutes. Emig's survey of sixteen professional writers indicated that only one out of four developed elaborate outlines before writing, but that most developed informal outlines comprised of words and phrases.[12] McKee surveyed eighty technical writers to detemine how extensively outlining was used.[13] Responses indicated that they developed topic outlines before writing, but that outlines were usually made up of only words and phrases. Only four writers in McKee's study developed formal sentence outlines. These studies indicate that outlining before writing is useful to students and professional writers, but insisting on development of formal sentence outlines is of questionable value.

Writing As A Process

As indicated above, effective writers usually engage in some thoughtful planning before they begin to write. They also revise and rewrite what they have written. Revisions often include changes in content, paragraph organization, and sentence structure—not just surface features such as spelling. If we are to help children become effective writers, it is important, then, to teach writing as a process. This process should include **prewriting, writing,** and **rewriting**.

Prewriting activities may include talking, reading, and thinking about the subject matter. They should result in a preliminary outline, possibly consisting of nothing more than a list of words or phrases. Location of any needed sources of information and securing that information are also legitimate prewriting activities.

Writing should result in the first draft or rough draft. During this phase, emphasis is on expression of ideas, with minimal concern for correctness of spelling and other surface features.

Rewriting begins with an oral reading of the rough draft. This should enable the writer to discover desirable changes in content, and to identify any needed changes in sentence and paragraph structure. A second draft is written, then read aloud again to identify any further changes. Additional drafts may be written. Once the writer is satisfied with her content and organization, she then checks for usage, spelling, and mechanics. A final draft is then written, incorporating all changes.

Close supervision of children's writing efforts during this process, particularly those of beginning writers, is *very* important. Children simply do not initially possess the organizational skills and self-discipline requisite to good writing. These must be learned. It is usually necessary to pace the children's efforts by setting reasonable deadlines, and to supervise their progress by checking their effort at each stage of this process. Just checking the final paper will not do.

Revising Strategies

The poor writer, regardless of his age, tends to procrastinate, to avoid writing when possible. When he realizes that he **has** to write, he hurriedly "completes" the task. Little or no planning occurs before writing. He simply begins writing. A thought is written, then he thinks about what to say next. Then another thought is written—and so on. This is the classic "what next" approach to writing. Revision is resisted. When he does revise his material, he may simply recopy it more neatly without making any changes in the message. Sometimes he unknowingly inserts more errors. At best, he corrects a few errors in spelling, punctuation, or other surface features. His materials are brief and usually more difficult to understand because they are not well organized, sometimes even omit needed information.

Based on her examinations of third graders' revising strategies, Calkins identified four developmental levels: **random, refining, transition**, and **interacting**.[14] **Random** revisers simply write successive drafts without examining earlier drafts. Any changes are accidental or arbitrary. When asked to insert new information, it is added at the end, regardless of appropriateness. **Refiners** usually limit changes to cosmetics or words, and occasionally addition of sentences. They will retain at least 75 percent of their earlier drafts. **Transition** revisers are not satisfied with making copies of earlier drafts or revising. They usually begin another draft when they rewrite, retaining little of the earlier draft. When asked to insert new information, they reread and insert the information in an appropriate place. **Interacting** revisers use a variety of symbols to indicate changes on a rough draft and use the earlier draft as a springboard to new ideas.

Stallard's study of "good student writers" tends to support these findings.[15] In addition to finding that these writers spent considerably more time in prewriting activities than randomly selected writers, he reported that they also made more revisions per paper. He reported that they averaged over twelve revisions per paper while those of the other group averaged only four per paper. Revision is obviously an essential component of effective writing!

Dealing With The Dislike of Rewriting

Let's face it! No one **enjoys** having to rewrite a paper again and again. Children are no exception. There is often an on-going struggle between the teacher who recognizes the importance of revision and rewriting, and her pupils who dislike doing it. Development of a sense of audience can, however, help children appreciate the importance of rewriting and accept it as a necessary step in the writing process. But they will not **enjoy** doing it.

There is a solution! Word processors and printers! After making her revisions on the screen, all the writer has to do is press "save" and she has saved her revised draft. Making a final copy is as simple as directing the printer to print a copy. Fortunately, many schools now have such equipment on hand. The question is: Do students have ample opportunities to **use** it? Ideally, there should be enough word processors and printers available so students don't have to wait in line for access. The importance of this equipment to the writing program cannot be overstated! It facilitates revision and makes production of new copies **much** easier. Student resistence to rewriting is virtually eliminated. An added benefit is efficiency. This hardware significantly reduces the amount of time a student needs to arrive at his final copy. More writing can be accomplished in a given time period!

Developing Children's Imagery

An important ingredient of good narrative writing, especially stories, is imagery. That is, selecting and arranging descriptive words that will enable the reader to visualize the scenes, people, things, events, and other important elements in the story. The task of the writer, then, is to choose words and carefully arrange them so his readers will develop appropriate visual images and feelings as they read. He paints pictures with words. As his readers become engrossed in the story, they "see a movie" as they **experience** the story. Good narrative writing, then, enables the reader not just to recognize and understand words. It is more than just "complete" sentences. It can reveal a character's intermost thoughts, his most secret fears. It enables the reader to "feel" the story.

Development of imagery in writing doesn't occur overnight. Children, especially young children, tend to write in a manner similar to Joe Friday's speech. They just give the facts—and these facts are usually the bare facts. Their writing naturally lacks the detail, color, and feelings found in literature published for children. Children include the basic events, a few descriptive words, and use "said" repeatedly to introduce quotes. Imagery must be taught!

How do teachers help children develop imagery in their writing? Sentence expansion exercises are often used with young children to demonstrate how to write a more descriptive sentence. These teachers frequently ask their pupils how places, things, and characters in their stories look, smell, taste, feel, and sound. Children also practice describing pictures, objects, and other stimuli. They examine how authors create images in selected stories from their literature. My students and I also developed a list of descriptive words, such as *muttered*, that could be substituted for *said*. This list is included in Chapter 5.

Handwriting Problems

Observation of writers will usually reveal two rather common handwriting habits that hinder writing efficiency: the *fishhook* technique, and holding the writing instrument in an awkward manner. These habits are formed during kindergarten and first grade and, once formed, are difficult to change.

The *fishhook* is used only by left-handed writers. Typically, the fishhook writer tilts his paper to the left, leans excessively over his desk, and *curls* his writing arm around his paper with a downward bend at the wrist. His writing hand and pen are positioned above the line where he is writing, and his pen is pointing toward the bottom edge of his paper. Yes, you've observed even prominent people using this technique. President Ford and President Carter are both fishhookers. But there's no reason for anyone to be saddled with this less efficient writing technique for the rest of his life.

What causes left-handed writers to develop this awkward, more fatiguing technique? Kindergarten and first grade teachers who forget to provide *different* instructions for left-handed writers—or who don't supervise their "lefties" close enough to make sure that they are using the appropriate technique! The lefties subsequently position their papers as the right-handed writers position theirs, slanting it to the left. But when the lefty attempts to write, his hand blocks his view of where he is writing. How does he remedy this problem? The *fishhook!* It allows him to maintain his paper position and see where he is writing. How can kindergarten and first grade teachers prevent this problem? Remember to **insist** that lefties tilt their papers to the right—and observe that they develop a habit of doing so from the beginning.

Observation of a typical group of seventh graders in the act of writing will also usually reveal that some are very creative in terms of how they hold their pens. Some hold their pens in ways that are obviously more fatiguing than the technique commonly prescribed in commercially-available handwriting programs. How can development of this habit be prevented? Kindergarten and first grade teachers need to demonstrate the proper technique and **insist** that their pupils develop the habit of using it from the beginning.

Evaluating and Grading Compositions

Evaluating student performance and reporting student progress are, of course, integral parts of an instructional program in writing. How teachers carry out these tasks is crucial to each child's development as a writer and to the success of the program. Improper practices in these areas can greatly limit the effectiveness of the writing program, no matter how often the children write, how many good stimuli are available, or how many extra prep periods the teacher is provided.

Perhaps one of the most important things to remember about evaluating student compositions is **not** to do it every time a child writes. We should sometimes respond as an audience—just enjoy their writing. Responding as an audience will communicate the real purpose of writing to the child and free her of the constant pressure of teacher appraisal and grades. Otherwise, the child will soon believe that we write for grades rather than for communication of ideas and enjoyment.

Types of Evaluation. A student's composition can be evaluated in terms of his unique rate of growth, focusing on his strengths and weaknesses, or in comparison with what is usually expected of children at his grade or age level. A comprehensive assessment of a child's development as a writer will necessarily include judgments based on both levels. Teachers are usually expected to report how the child's writing abilities compare with those of his peers, and also report how he is doing in terms of **his** rate of progress. Instructional feedback to the child, however, should be based on his abilities and what can be reasonably expected of him—not his classmates.

he will be frustrated by excessive negative feedback if he is below grade
unchallenged if he is above level.

ent compositions are usually evaluated in two different ways: **holistic
scoring** and **specific-response evaluations**. In either case, judgments are made
according to previously identified criteria, with a unique set for each type of material.
Occasionally, papers may be examined according to universal criteria—such as
vocabulary, types of sentence structures, and number of words per T-unit.
A form that I used with my students is included in Chapter 4.

Holistic scoring requires the evaluator to read an essay and rate its quality
according to a scale. This scoring method proceeds rather quickly because the
evaluator merely writes a number on the paper that indicates the overall rating
assigned to that paper. No comments or corrective feedback is written on the essay.
This method of scoring is frequently used by judges of writing contests and by
teachers who need to get an overall appraisal of their students' abilities. It is of little
immediate instructional value to the student since it provides no specific feedback to
him.

Specific-response evaluations require the evaluator to read an essay and to
provide feedback to the writer that focuses on specific elements. This method
proceeds rather slowly because the evaluator must read the material carefully and
write appropriate feedback on the paper. The feedback includes compliments for the
inclusion of desirable qualities and suggests or illustrates how to improve the
material. This method of evaluating student compositions is of considerable value to
the student since it provides positive feedback and useful corrective feedback about
specific items—not generalizations or just numbers.

The Nature of Feedback. What kind of feedback best facilitates the child's
development as a writer? Schroeder's study of the effects of **positive feedback,
corrective feedback,** and **no feedback** on fourth graders provides some clues.[16] In
his study, children were randomly divided into the three appropriate groups, then
required to write two compositions each week for a fourteen week period. "Positive"
comments praised desirable features that were included. "Corrective" comments
identified the absence of desirable features and illustrated how they could have been
included. Examination of the compositions revealed that students in the **positive** and
corrective feedback groups performed at a significantly higher level than those in
the **no feedback** group. Students in the **corrective feedback** group performed
slightly better than those in the **positive feedback** group.

My experiences support these findings. A teacher's feedback should be constructive in nature. She should provide positive feedback and corrective feedback as
needed. Positive feedback consists of compliments or praise for desirable elements
included in the material. It is important to all writers, but especially to kindergarteners
and first graders. Corrective feedback identifies errors or omissions, and suggests or
demonstrates how to correct them. Negative feedback, which consists of sarcasm,

other critical comments, and identification of errors without accompanying helpful questions, suggestions,or corrections, should be avoided.

Essentially, then, feedback should include both positive feedback and corrective feedback. Second, it should focus on specific items. While responses like, "Very good," and "I like your story," are well received by pupils seeking teacher approval, they are of no real *instructional* value to older students who are trying to improve their writing. Specificity will tell the writer exactly what feature is missing or how one needs to be changed, and it will reduce the possibility that the writer will interpret a comment as a criticism of him rather than how something was written. Third, feedback should show the student *how* to improve something—not just point out an error. Fourth, feedback should be tailored to the needs and sensitivity of each child. The amount of feedback, then, will vary according to each child's developmental level, his specific needs, and his ability to accept and use it. And finally, feedback should also focus on the adequacy of content—not just spelling and mechanics.

Promptness. How soon should a teacher provide feedback to a student about a composition? As soon as possible. Prompt feedback is more meaningful and beneficial since it focuses on something still fresh in the child's memory. Delayed feedback, on the other hand, will extend student anxiety about grades and be less meaningful. It may also cause the student to conclude that the teacher considered the writing assignment to be unimportant.

Adequate Teacher Prep Time. Requiring a child to write a composition obligates the teacher to respond conscientiously as an evaluator. The problem is: finding the time. Traditionally, teachers have been provided a single prep period each day, or five class periods per week, for the purpose of meeting a variety of responsibilities such as planning lessons, grading papers, conferring with other school peronnel and parents, and preparing materials for class. One prep period is simply not adequate for writing teachers. Although the time needed to grade compositions will vary because of several factors, teachers generally need *at least* ten minutes to evaluate and grade a child's composition in a thoughtful, conscientious manner. This includes time for two readings of the composition: first, for judging the adequacy and organization of information for the writer's intended purpose(s), then for examing specific items such as grammar, mechanics, and spelling. For a class of 25 students, this amounts to about four hours! This does not include time needed for examining and providing feedback on rough drafts and carrying out managerial tasks such as classifying student errors on a checklist or filing sample compositions in students' folders. Assuming that a class will write one composition each week, the teacher should be provided with at least four hours of prep time each week for evaluating and grading students' compositions, and additional time for responding to rough drafts and carrying out various managerial tasks. Otherwise, writing teachers will have to continue spending much of their after-school time evaluating compositions—which they increasingly seem unwilling to do.

Efficiency in Evaluating. Several practices can help teachers deal with the reality of limited prep time. Not grading every composition a student writes is one. This lightens the grading load on the teacher and, as pointed out above, lessens the pressure of grades on pupils.

Viewing evaluation as a joint responsibility of the teacher and the pupil is another way of dealing with the reality of limited prep time. In addition, it can also contribute to the success of the writing program. Since not all materials should be graded, then, the student can be given the option of selecting some of those that are graded. This will place him in the role as an appraiser of his writing. In doing so, he will help the teacher identify his growing edge since he will obviously select what he believes are his best works.

Another way students can help carry the burden of evaluating compositions is through peer evaluations. My students always seemed to enjoy proofreading each other's drafts and offering helpful suggestions for improvements. This activity also helped meet their need to interact with each other.

Evaluating papers according to standards or criteria can also lighten the burden of grading. Such standards facilitate evaluation by guiding the evaluator's efforts. There is another benefit: They facilitate student writing by providing direction *during* writing and revising efforts. To be most beneficial, these criteria or standards of desirable qualities should be generated with the students during class discussions prior to writing, then displayed on a chart during writing. Generation of standards in this manner enables students to understand more clearly the nature of the material they are to write, and it helps them understand how the material will be evaluated.

One practice that provides for individual differences also facilitates evaluation. In the typical sixth grade class, for example, there are usually a few writers who are clearly below grade level. What to do! First, be realistic in our expectations. Holding a sixth grader to sixth grade level expectations is unrealistic if he is developmentally a fourth grader. Assuming that his self-confidence is shaky, he needs to experience success. When evaluating this child's composition, check his paper for only one or two types of errors, such as staying on the topic in a paragraph or writing "complete" sentences. Sometimes, even ask this student what he would like you to check. Otherwise, he will likely be overwhelmed with the variety and frequency of errors identified in his writing.

The Problem of Bias. Beginning with the development of IQ tests early in this century, considerable attention focused on development of "standardized" instruments that were designed to measure various student attributes. The primary criteria guiding the development of these instruments were: validity, reliability, and fairness. These tests had to be impartial and consistently yield *unbiased* data—regardless of who administered them. Thus was born the "objective" test composed of multiple-choice, true/false and matching items. Following the lead of the IQ tests, it was assumed that achievement tests had to be "objective" if they were to yield unbiased data. This resulted in the development of countless achievement tests in various subject areas that were composed of similar types of test items.

Assessment of children's development as writers, however, has proved to be a more difficult task. Obviously, the only way to assess a child's ability to write is to examine samples of his writing. But troubling questions arose about reliability and fairness. Earlier IQ tests and achievement tests were designed to produce quantified results: numbers. If assessment was to be fair and impartial, how could assessment of writing samples be quantified? One result is the writing scale. This instrument requires the evaluator to compare a sample of a child's writing with samples on a scale that range from poor to excellent. The evaluator must identify the sample on the scale that most closely resembles the sample being evaluated. Another attempt to quantify assessment requires, for example, calculating the average number of words per T-unit. One might even determine the ratios of simple, compound, and complex sentence patterns. Such assessments produce objective data.

These objective data are useful when conducting a comprehensive assessment of a child's development as a writer. Some subjective information based more heavily on the evaluator's judgment, however, is also useful—especially when determining a child's development in terms of *his* abilities. The problem is: How can evaluator bias be minimized?

Early in my teaching career, I discovered that it took me less time to grade a set of compositions when I knew which student wrote each paper. Apparently, after grading two or three compositions of a student, I determined his writing capabilities and expected him to perform accordingly. I then realized that I was injecting bias into my grading. It was so easy to see what I *expected* to see. A study by Harari and McDavid tends to support this.[17] They asked a group of teachers to grade student essays that were equal in quality. Different first names had been written on the identical papers. They reported that essays with names like David and Michael received grades that were a full letter higher than those with names like Elmer and Hubert. Girls' names revealed a similar difference. Now what?

One practice that helps minimize bias is evaluating papers anonymously. That is, the evaluator evaluates a composition without knowledge of who wrote it. There is a place for this practice. When evaluating student performance in terms of minimum standards or grade level expectations, we must compare a student's writing with those standards, not his standards. We need to evaluate papers anonymously so that we are not influenced by what we have previously learned to expect from that child. This enables us to judge the adequacy of his development according to those arbitrary standards.

Basing evaluations on specific criteria or standards can also reduce bias. This requires the evaluator to examine a composition according to *previously* identified desirable qualities. He must determine to what extent it meets those standards. The criteria guide the evaluator's judgments by reminding him what to consider.

One of the criticisms sometimes leveled at teachers is that they "grade down" student compositions when student opinions expressed in compositions differ from theirs. The possibility of this happening can be minimized in three ways. First, the teacher should allow, even encourage her pupils to feel free to express their opinions and rationales on issues examined in class. Second, she should conscientiously adhere to previously identified criteria when evaluating compositions. And third, she should be sensitive to her own feelings and attitudes and remain on alert for emergence of any prejudices in her judgments.

Proofreading for Spelling

Beginning teachers are sometimes alarmed by the frequency and persistence of spelling errors in children's writing—especially in the writing of young children. They needn't be alarmed. Until children have developed a sizeable sight vocabulary and correct sound-letter associations, they spell words phonetically. This results in numerous spelling errors since about half of the words in the English language are not spelled phonetically.

Correct spelling, of course, should be a concern of the writer since his reader will usually notice misspelled words quickly—and judge him accordingly. The problem is: *When* should the writer be concerned with spelling words correctly? Checking the spellings of words definitely should be one of the *last* tasks in writing a paper, not one of the first. Otherwise, as is often the case, the child may become preoccupied with spelling in his initial draft when he should be focusing on expressing his ideas, saying what he means.

When it is appropriate to check for spelling errors, we often proofread material without recognizing misspelled words. This occurs because of our natural tendency to focus on meanings in sentences as we read rather than on the spelling of individual words. A much more effective technique is to read each line backwards—that is, from right to left. The proofreader can no longer read meanings in sentences; he focuses on individual words. To minimize repeated misspellings of words, encourage each pupil to maintain a list of his misspelled words for future reference and study.

Why not simply encourage children to use the "spell check" in the word processing program? That's fine. But we must remember that the spell check merely identifies the misspelled word, then lists three or four possible correct replacements from which the writer must choose. Spell check, then, still requires the writer to be able to recognize the correct spelling of the word, or, at the very least, requires him to go to a source that can provide that information. Obviously, it is advantageous for the writer to have a basic sight vocabulary of spelling words. Otherwise, since about half of the words in the English language are spelled phonetically, the beginning writer will typically misspell numerous words. But even accomplished writers will misspell words. We can't avoid proofreading our material for spelling errors—even with the aid of a spell check program.

NOTES

1. Steven Kellogg, How A Picture Book Is Made: The Island Of The Skog, The Signature Collection (Weston, CN: Weston Woods Studios, 1976), filmstrip/tape.

2. George Hillocks, Jr., Research on Written Composition: New Directions for Teaching (Urbana, IL: ERIC Clearinghouse on Reading and Communication Skills, 1986), 192-204.

3. Hillocks, Jr., 204-17.

4. Franklin S. Hoyt, "Studies in English Grammar," College Record 7 (1906): 467-500.

5. Frank O'Hare, Sentence Combining: Improving Student Writing Without Formal Grammar Instruction, Research Report no. 15. (Urbana, IL: National Council of Teachers of English, 1973).

6. Lucy McCormick Calkins and Donald H. Graves, "When Children Want to Punctuate: Basic Skills Belong In Context," Language Arts 57 (May 1980): 567-73.

7. Calkins and Graves, 572-73.

8. Lester S. Golub and Wayne C. Fredrick, "An Analysis of Children's Writing Under Different Stimulus Conditions," Research in The Teaching of English 4, no. 2 (February 1970): 168-80.

9. Gordon Brossell, "Rhetorical Specifications in Essay Examination Topics," College English 45, no. 2 (February 1983): 165-73.

10. Ruth Ann Beeker, "The Effects of Oral Planning on Fifth-Grade Composition," Dissertation Abstracts International 30, no. 11 (1970): 4870-A.

11. Charles K. Stallard, Jr., "An Analysis of the Writing Behavior of Good Student Writers," Dissertation Abstracts International 33, no. 7 (1973): 3408-A.

12. Janet Emig, "The Composing Process of Twelfth Graders," (Urbana, IL: National Council of Teachers of English, 1971), ED 058 205.

13. Blaine K. McKee, "Types of Outlines Used by Technical Writers," Journal of English Teaching Techniques 7, no. 4 (Winter 1974/1975): 30-36.

14. Lucy McCormick Calkins, "Children's Rewriting Strategies," Research in The Teaching of English 14, no. 4 (December 1980): 331-41.

15. Stallard, Jr., 3408-A.

16. Thomas Steven Schroeder, "The Effects of Positive and Corrective Written Teacher Feedback on Selected Writing Behaviors of Fourth-Grade Children," Dissertation Abstracts International 34, no. 6 (1973): 2935-A.

17. Herbert Harari and John W. McDavid, "Name Stereotypes and Teachers' Expectations," Journal of Educational Psychology 65, no. 2 (October 1973): 222-25.

CHAPTER 4: DEVELOPING THE WRITING PROGRAM

Development, implementation, and management of the writing program requires decisions regarding the following:

1. **Determination of the Priority on Writing**
2. **Establishment of Desired Goals and Specific Objectives**
3. **Assessment of the Current Status of Student Skills**
4. **Assignment of the Necessary Resources to the Program**
5. **Identification of Effective Teaching Methods and Learning Experiences**
6. **Assignment of Goals, Objectives, and Learning Experiences to Instructional Levels**
7. **Evaluating Pupil Achievement and Program Effectiveness**
8. **Implementing the Writing Program**
9. **Managing the Writing Program**

Each of these tasks is described in this chapter; or, as in the case of the curriculum, for example, the reader is referred to another chapter where the task is addressed.

Determination of The Priority on Writing

Establishment of an appropriate priority should be based on consideration of several factors. These have been described in chapters 1 and 2. In brief, they include:

1. The Importance of Writing in Today's World
2. The Relative Difficulty of Becoming an Effective Writer
3. The Current Status of the Students' Writing Skills
4. Consideration of the Various Demands on the Available Resources

In Teacher Training Programs

In teacher training programs, priorities are usually stated or implied in mission statements, college catalogues, and various departmental materials. These priorities are, of course, based on guidelines specified by the state and various accrediting agencies. Programs are designed so that they supposedly offer students realistic opportunities to accomplish specific occupational and professional goals within the parameters of the total credit hours for a degree. Upon completion of the program, the student is supposedly prepared to assumed a specific occupational or professional role.

As pointed out in Chapter 1, the teacher training program that is designed to enable students to become elementary school teachers typically requires students to complete various foundation courses, and curriculum and methods courses. Each curriculum and methods course focuses on a specific subject area, such as math or social studies. The training students receive to enable them to be writing teachers is often limited to a language arts course. This course typically includes study of the nature of language, how children acquire language, oral expression, listening, grammar and usage, handwriting, spelling, and written composition. Attention to written composition is usually limited to only 8 to 12 hours of instruction. This is grossly inadequate! It is unrealistic to expect college students with only 8 to 12 hours of instruction about teaching writing to be competent writing teachers!

How has the current program been justified? Some have argued that the basic composition courses in the English Department that students are also required to complete provide the needed additional training. This is nonsense. These courses are designed to develop or to improve students' writing skills. Students are required to write, write, and write. But the extent to which they help students improve their writing is debatable. Class sizes and teaching loads usually preclude supervised revisions of materials. The prof does well just to grade the final version. Even worse, students are sometimes given a writing topic at the beginning of the period and required to hand in a paper by the end of the period—for a grade! These courses, then, not only result in limited improvement of students' writing skills, they sometimes teach how *not* to teach writing! Yes, the competent writing teacher should be an effective writer. But even if these courses did enable all students to become highly effective writers, this would not be enough. Preparation to teach **children** how to write also requires attention to:

> Understanding the Nature of Writing
> The Importance of Writing
> The Current Status of Writing Skills
> The Developmental Stages of Becoming a Writer
> The Writing Curriculum
> Various Aspects of the Teacher's Role
> Building Positive Attitudes Toward Writing
> The Role of Children's Literature in the Writing Program
> Effective Prewriting Activities for Children

Effective Writing Practices for Children
Evaluating and Grading Children's Writing
Writing in a Whole Language Program
Implementation and Management of the Writing Program

The current state of children's and adults' writing skills is a sad testimonial, in part, to the inadequacy of current program requirements. How can we justify requiring students to complete two courses in reading while limiting instruction in written composition to only a portion of one course? We can't! As pointed out earlier, reading is an inherently easier task than writing, and writing skills are notoriously worse than reading skills. Many students, through no fault of their own, are simply not being adequately trained to teach children to write!

What needs to be done? A higher priority on writing would more realistically reflect the current needs, the complex nature of writing, and the difficulty of becoming an effective writer. Degree and teacher certification requirements need to be expanded so considerably more instructional time to train students to be writing teachers can be provided. Instructional time at least equal to that provided for reading is easily justified. This could be achieved by (a) expanding the current language arts course, (b) removing some of the content from the current language arts course and including it in a separate course, or (c) requiring additional language arts courses so adequate instructional time is provided for written composition.

In Elementary Schools

In the typical elementary school curriculum today, writing is included in the language arts instructional period. Handwriting, spelling, and those other areas noted above are also included in this instructional period. Time for writing is, of course, limited because of the amount of subject matter included in this period.

The existing arrangement usually provides writing teachers with the same amount of prep time as teachers of other subject areas—even though evaluating and grading written composition is the most time-consuming evaluative task. This inequity is compounded in departmentalized arrangements where the English teacher is assigned a full load—with even more written compositions to grade!

And what kind of priority has resulted in these conditions? Just ask school administrators about their priority on writing. Without exception, they will state that a high priority is placed on teaching children to write in their schools. Such statements are usually for PR purposes—and may reflect misunderstandings about the complex nature of writing and amount of instructional time needed. Placing a high priority on writing, on the one hand, while providing the usual amount of time for writing instruction and assigning full teaching loads to writing teachers is contradictory.

What needs to be done? A **serious** commitment to writing will include adequate time for writing teachers to complete most, if not all, of their evaluating and grading tasks at school. Otherwise, teachers are going to be reluctant to include sufficient writing experiences and feedback to students. Teaching loads of writing teachers need to be reduced by at least one-third. Such a commitment will also provide at least as much class time for writing instruction as is provided for reading instruction so children can write and receive useful feedback each week.

Establishing Goals and Objectives

In schools where the commercially-available language arts program is the writing program, decisions about curriculum have already been made—regardless of the shortcomings of the program. It is recommended here, as implied above, that local schools consider developing their own writing program, or, at the very least, consider the commercially-available program only as a base from which to expand. In such case, the professional staff will need to consider the following:
1. The priority on writing in the total school curriculum
2. The priority on writing in the language arts program
3. Concepts and skills related to effective writing
4. Types of materials that the student will likely be expected to write during his lifetime
5. Realistic expectations about the learning abilities of the students
6. Resources and expectations unique to the local community

For direction when establishing goals and objectives, refer to Chapter 6. Purposes of writing, types of materials often written by children and adults, and concepts and skills related to writing are included in that chapter.

Assessment of The Current Status of Student Skills

This task is accomplished by (1) examining records about previous growth, and (2) conducting a preliminary examination at the beginning of the school year. These tasks should be carried out whenever a writing program is being developed or improved and by the classroom teacher at the beginning of the school year. Information describing how the preliminary examination can be carried out is provided later in this chapter.

Assignment of Resources to The Program

Resources include personnel, time, space, equipment, and various teaching aids and materials. Assignment of these resources depends, of course, on the priority placed on writing, the availablility of resources, and the specific goals and objectives in the program. It also requires consideration of the total resources of the school and the demands placed on them by the total school curriculum. At a minimum, resources for the writing program should include:
1. Reduced teaching loads for teachers
2. Sufficient class time each week for students to complete a writing experience in class

11. **Peer assistance is part of student learning activities.** Students occasionally have opportunities to assist each other during the writing process. Appropriate criteria provide direction for this assistance. This practice capitalizes on children's need to interact, and also contributes to the development of a sense of audience.

12. **The teacher is a writer, facilitator, and an audience, not just an evaluator or judge.** She models both an interest in writing and an ability to write, creates a favorable environment for writing, serves as an assistant to students when they are writing, and enjoys reading and listening to their materials.

13. **Writing stimuli are used to stimulate children's writing interests.** Pictures, objects, provocative questions or statements about relevant concerns, editorials, newspaper headlines and articles, story frameworks, titles and story beginnings and endings are used to stimulate children's writing.

14. **Early writing experiences are integrated with early reading experiences.** This is accomplished first in the dictated group experience story, then in the personal experience story.

15. **Writing is emphasized across the curriculum.** Children have opportunities to apply their writing skills and receive useful feedback in various subject areas.

16. **Writing is taught as a developmental process.** Fundamental to the writing strategy is recognition that writing is a developmental process. The task of the teacher is to determine each child's developmental level at the beginning of the school year and form realistic expectations for each child.

17. **Teachers demonstrate sensitivity and fairness in evaluating and grading materials.** Evaluating/grading materials is constructive in nature, it is prompt, and it focuses on specific items. Evaluation of a composition is based on (a) previously identified criteria and (b) the student's unique developmental status as a writer. Feedback is tailored to each student's needs and to his ability to accept and apply it.

18. **Feedback to students is constructive.** Feedback consists of positive statements—pointing out desirable qualities included in their writing, and corrective feedback—specific suggestions that illustrate how a material can be improved.

19. **An efficient management system is used.** It facilitates completion of teaching tasks, such as evaluating compositions. It also facilitates storage and retrieval of information that indicates each child's development as a writer, and enables the teacher to review quickly a child's progress when planning writing experiences or when preparing for conferences with the student or his parents.

20. **Ample supplies, aids, and equipment are apparent.** These typically range from dictionaries and literary works, on the one hand, to file cabinets, overhead projectors, and word processors and printers on the other.

provide some indication of the child's maturity as a writer, but are, of course, inadequate in themselves. This type of evaluation could be recorded on a form like the one below that I developed for use with my students.

PERIODIC ASSESSMENT OF BASIC WRITING SKILLS

Student:_____ Level:_____ Date: _____

Description of Sample: _____

          Poor   Serve As A Model

Ratings: 1...................................6

Criteria   **Rating**

VOCABULARY .... _____
Comments: _____
_____

SENTENCE STRUCTURE
    Words per T-unit_____
    Ratio of simple/compound/complex_____
Comments: _____
_____

CLARITY OF STATEMENTS .... _____

Comments: _____
_____
_____

PARAGRAPH DEVELOPMENT
    Clearness of main ideas .... _____
    Adequacy of details .... _____
    Relevancy of statements .... _____
    Flow of ideas within .... _____
    Transitions .... _____

Comments: _____
_____
_____

continued on next page

EXPRESSIVENESS
Originality/colorfulness .... _____
Ratio of modifiers to nouns/
    pronouns/verbs .... _____
Symbolism .... _____

Comments: _____
_____
_____

MECHANICS
Handwriting neatness .... _____
Spelling .... _____
Capitalization
    Beginning of sentence .... _____
    Proper names .... _____
Punctuation
    Terminal marks .... _____
    Within sentences .... _____
Grammar and usage
    Agreement in number between
        subject and verb .... _____
    Point of view .... _____
    Agreement in number between
        pronoun and antecedent. .... _____
    Pronoun case .... _____
    Verb tense .... _____
    Clarity of referents .... _____
    Absence of other nonstandard forms
        or word choice confusions .... _____

Comments: _____
_____
_____
_____
_____

These assessments by individual teachers should be augmented every third year with the writing section of the school-wide standardized test. These usually require comparison of a specific type of sample of the child's writing, such as a descriptive paragraph, with samples provided on a scale.

Ultimately, program effectiveness is measured by pupil achievement—how well the pupils are developing as writers. However, program characteristics such as those described earlier in this chapter are useful indicators of program effectiveness. A checklist, such as the following **ASSESSMENT OF THE WRITING PRO-GRAM,** beginning on page 59, can help determine the priority placed on written composition and the extent to which effective conditions and practices are in place. The most highly recommended elements are marked on the following checklist with an asterisk (*). To use the instrument, simply write 1 in the space provided for each item that is included in the program, and write 0 if it cannot be accounted for on a regular basis. A total of 49 points is possible.

Implementing the Writing Program

We've all heard stories about teachers requiring their students to write a composition at the beginning of the year that focused on what they did last summer. Students typically dislike this assignment and often just sit—trying to think of something to write about. Their initial response is often, "I didn't do nothin'." This assignment is supposed to provide the teacher with insight into the child's writing abilities and recent experiences. It falls flat because the assignment is too broad, and there is no attempt to stimulate student thinking prior to writing. This is no way to begin the writing program—even though the teacher's objective is worthwhile.

The above assignment can be salvaged. Instead of just telling students to write a theme that told about what they did last summer, I began writing a list of things that **I** did during the summer. These were very specific and were shown to the students via the overhead projector as I generated the list. I typically included mundane items, such as mowing the lawn and vacuuming the house, as well as more exciting experiences, such as riding in a hot air balloon, doing something "dumb," and getting angry at another driver. This list not only stimulated children's thinking about their own summer experiences, it enabled them to be become better acquainted with me as a person. The following list was developed by me at the beginning of one school year.

1. Changed oil and filter in my truck
2. Washed the car
3. Rode in a hot air balloon
4. Flew to Miami, Florida, then on a cruise ship to Nassau, Bahamas
5. Bought/rode my four-wheeler
6. Fed my sheep each day
7. Recaptured a ram that got out of the pasture

ASSESSMENT OF THE WRITING PROGRAM

THE STUDENTS:

_____ *Write materials each week.

_____ *Participate in discussions about criteria and scales before writing.

_____ *Occasionally assist each other during the rewriting phase of the writing process.

_____ *Have opportunities to share their materials in class.

_____ *Practice development of foundation skills.

_____ *Examine materials in children's literature in order to gain insight into writing problems.

_____ *Engage in appropriate prewriting activities prior to writing each material.

_____ *Consider appropriate criteria for each material before writing.

_____ *Write and revise at least two drafts of each material.

_____ *Check for errors in spelling and mechanics in the final phase of the writing process.

THE TEACHER:

_____ *Communicates to pupils the historical significance of writing at the beginning of the year.

_____ *Communicates the importance of writing in the world today in a variety of ways.

_____ *Emphasizes writing rather than studying grammar and countless pages of workbook practice on mechanics.

_____ *Promotes the act of writing as a process that includes specific tasks in a particular sequence.

_____ *Emphasizes ideas more than spelling and mechanics, especially in initial drafts.

continued on next page

_____ *Provides scales/criteria or helps students develop scales/criteria for each material before writing.

_____ *Writes and shares with her pupils some of the same types of materials that she expects them to write.

_____ *Provides prompt praise and constructive feedback for each child.

_____ *Occasionally responds just as an audience to students' writings.

_____ *Guides study and appreciation of selections from literature that illustrate specific writing elements.

_____ *Includes writing experiences across the curriculum.

_____ *Integrates reading, literature, language mechanics, usage, spelling, handwriting, sentence sense, and paragraph sense with writing to some extent.

_____ Supervises writing club, writing contests, class/school newspaper.

_____ *Adjusts expectations and challenges each pupil according to his developmental status as a writer.

_____ Writes proofreading practice material for pupils.

_____ *Arranges publication of pupils' writings in newspaper, library.

_____ *Arranges field trips to local businesses, such as printers, publishers, and the newspaper, to illustrate the importance of writing.

_____ Arranges for resource people,such as authors, editors, and columnists, to visit class.

_____ *Uses a management system to keep track of each pupil's development as a writer.

CLASSROOM ENVIRONMENT:

_____ *A writing center is provided.

_____ *Student compositions are displayed.

_____ *Provides ample time for pupils to complete writing experiences.

_____ *A step-by-step process for writing is displayed.

continued on next page

_____ *A "Checklist for Improving My Writing" is displayed.

_____ *Student compositions are bound and housed in classroom or school library.

_____ *Posters showing appropriate criteria, "Say What You Mean," and "Confusing Words Unconfused" are displayed.

THE SCHOOL:

_____ *Writing is clearly identified as a high priority by school board and administration.

_____ *The building administrator occasionally visits classes, listens attentively and praises pupils when they share their writings.

_____ *A comprehensive writing curriculum is published.

_____ *Adequate fiscal support from local board is provided for reduced teaching loads, smaller classes, and extra prep time for writing teachers.

_____ *Adequate fiscal support from local board is provided for needed equipment and supplies.

_____ Pupils are provided opportunities to share their writings during school assemblies when appropriate.

_____ *Older students are encouraged to write stories and poems for younger pupils, and read these materials to those pupils.

_____ Pupils read their writings to school-parent organizations when appropriate.

_____ *Awards for writing are presented during school assemblies

_____ School writing contests are conducted.

_____ *Support for a school "authors' club" is provided.

_____ The school newspaper is largely written by students.

_____ *Writing is placed on an equal footing with reading in a variety of ways, such as a literacy specialist rather than just a reading specialist.

TOTAL POINTS: _____   (Desired: 49)
                    (Most highly recommended: 42)

8. Visited family
9. Spent the night in San Antonio
10. Attended a computer workshop
11. Mowed the lawn
12. Grew tomatoes
13. Floated down the Guadalupe River on innertubes with wife and friends
14. Rented a Jeep and located a ranch in Colorado where my dad and I killed a bear when I was in high school
15. Got angry at another driver who almost killed me
16. Rode a Concours (motorcycle)
17. Drove a Corvette
18. Visited friends in Ardmore, Oklahoma
19. Visited nephew in Waco, Texas
20. Hunted arrowheads
21. Went to the dentist
22. Went to the doctor about my right knee
23. Installed a fuel pump on my truck
24. Lost and found my wallet

My students invariably asked me to tell about some of the experiences, and I shared one orally. I then asked each of them to make a similar list. It became a contest to some to see who could make the longest list. Students often surprised themselves when they realized how many different things they did during the summer. This inventory served as a source of topics to write about throughout the year.

After they finished making their lists, I allowed them to share a few orally. I then asked each student to select one of his own experiences and write a story telling about it. I wrote a story about one of my experiences as they wrote about theirs. This first sample enabled me to appraise each student's writing abilities. I examined each according to the checklist beginning on page 63—but, of course, I did not grade these compositions. This initial sample and analysis were placed in the student's folder in a file cabinet.

Also important, especially at the beginning of the year, is an attractive, stimulating classroom environment. Bulletin board displays of previous students' writings, a writing center, and, for example, a poster outlining the writing process, all help communicate that writing is important.

Managing the Writing Program

Efficient management is an important element of program success in any subject area. It is, however, especially important in the writing program because of the maze of skills inherent in writing, the variety of writing problems children have, and the limited prep time often provided for writing teachers. Absence of such a system will complicate the teacher's assessments of student progress and seriously threaten the

PRELIMINARY ASSESSMENT OF STUDENT WRITING ABILITIES

Student: _____ Date: _____

THE WRITING PROCESS
Planning Before Writing (check one):

_____ No apparent planning; just starts writing, using the "what next" approach

_____ Minimal planning apparent in a rough, incomplete outline and some discussion or research

_____ Considerable planning apparent in a largely complete outline, some discussion and research

_____ Extensive planning apparent in a comprehensive outline, discussion and/or notes

Revising Strategy (check one):

_____ Merely recopies first draft; any changes are unintentional or for cosmetics; corrects no errors

_____ Retains at least 80% of first draft; makes an occasional change in sentences; corrects a few errors in spelling

_____ Makes a few significant changes in content/organization of sentences/ paragraphs; corrects most errors in spelling/usage/mechanics

_____ Makes several significant changes in content/organization of sentences/ paragraphs, resulting in very effective writing; corrects all or nearly all errors

THE MATERIAL

Serious Deficiency   Serve as a Model
Ratings: 1....................................6

Vocabulary. ...._____

Sentence Development
Completeness ...._____
Types. ...._____
Clarity.._____
Superfluous language. ...._____

continued on next page

Parallelism .... _____

Comments: _____

_____

_____

Paragraph Development
Clearness of main ideas .... _____
Adequacy of details .... _____
Relevancy of .... _____
Point of view .... _____
Variety of sentence beginnings .... _____
Variety in sentence length .... _____
Sequence of ideas .... _____
Transitions .... _____
Sequence of paragraphs .... _____

Comments: _____

_____

_____

Grammar and Usage
Agreement .... _____
Verb tense .... _____
Pronoun case .... _____
Clearness of pronoun reference .... _____
Modifier forms .... _____
Word choice .... _____

Comments: _____

_____

_____

Punctuation
End punctuation .... _____
Internal punctuation .... _____

Comments: _____

_____

_____

Capitalization
Sentence beginning .... _____
Internal capitalization .... _____
Titles .... _____

continued on next page

Comments: _____
_____
_____

Spelling. .... _____

Comments: _____
_____
_____

Handwriting
    Techniques .... _____
    Symbols .... _____

Comments: _____
_____
_____

What does effective management provide? It organizes and disciplines the use of time, space, equipment, materials, and personnel. It provides for the efficient use of space for records, materials, and equipment, and establishes routines for completing various teacher and learner tasks. Time allotments and deadlines facilitate completion of tasks such as evaluating and grading compositions. It also facilitates storage and retrieval of information that indicates each child's development as a writer. It enables the teacher to review quickly a child's progress when planning future writing experiences or when preparing for conferences with the student or her parents. File cabinets, folders, and planning books are essential.

A realistic understanding of the amount of time needed to complete writing tasks is very important. We need to remember that writing is a slow process. Students need time to complete this process in a thoughtful manner. If we rush them, the quality of their writing will suffer, and benefits of the writing experience will diminish. Although the amount of time needed to complete a writing task will vary because of several factors, students will usually need about a week to finish a composition. Post-writing activities, such as sharing what was written, class discussions about common difficulties, individual conferences with students, and completion of managerial tasks, will require additional time!

A writing center can also facilitate management of the writing program. With space and appropriate materials, it can help students function more independently, solving their own problems without leaning on the teacher every time a difficulty arises. What should be included in the center?
    Dictionaries
    Thesaurses

Almanacs
Crayons
Felt tip writing pens
Lined writing paper
Typing paper
Colored construction paper
Staplers
Rulers
Scissors
Hole punch
Transparent tape
Glue
Magazines
Wastebasket
File cabinet
Chalkboard
Free-standing easel with large unlined paper
Tape recorders

Word processors and printers may be housed elsewhere because of the amount of space they require.

Some practices that will lighten the management load and make control of the program easier are:

1. Don't grade everything your students write. Grade just enough to serve as a basis for the grading period.
2. Occasionally let your pupils check each other's papers during the writing process.
3. Don't get behind with your grading and managerial responsibilities. Set a deadline for grading each set of papers and completing the follow-up managerial tasks.
4. Set up a folder for each child.
5. Let your students file their papers in their folders.
6. Occasionally let your students classify their errors on the checklists.
7. Don't file everything a child writes. Just file enough samples to illustrate his progress as a writer.
8. Occasionally check a set of papers for only one or two types of errors—not everything that might be important or wrong.
9. Teach children how to use the word processor and the printer, and provide easy access to them in the writing center or other convenient place.

CHAPTER 5: STIMULATING CHILDREN TO WRITE

We teachers annually spend much time searching for ideas and materials that will arouse the interest of our students and create within them a desire to write. We strive to create a classroom environment that is interesting, challenging, and successful—one that is **writer friendly**. A writer friendly environment, however, is much more than an exciting writing activity or a colorful writing stimulus. The teacher's role, teaching methods, classroom arrangement and amenities, as well as specific writing experiences of children, are all vital components of this environment. Most of these have been addressed to a considerable extent in chapters 3 and 4.

In brief, the teacher is a writer, a facilitator, and an audience—not just an evaluator. She exhibits enthusiasm for writing and is genuinely interested in the materials her students create. She acknowledges that writing is not an easy task—even for professional writers—but demonstrates that it is a very worthy skill, one that serves practical needs and provides limitless enjoyment through literature, movies, and theater productions. She implements a strategy and writing experiences that facilitate children's development as writers.

This chapter will focus on (1) setting the stage for writing in the classroom, (2) helping children appreciate writing, and (3) specific writing activities that are effective and enjoyable to students.

Setting the Stage for Writing

The physical arrangement and amenities in the classroom can, of course, affect children's readiness for writing. The writing center is very important, but other materials can also stir children's interest in writing. Charts, such as the one listing the criteria for a particular type of material, are helpful. The charts below and on pages 69 and 70 seemed to help my middle school students during their writing efforts.

Other checklists described later in this chapter also seemed useful to my students. These charts would, of course, have to be simplified for children in the lower grades.

THE WRITING PROCESS

PREWRITING
    Reading
    Thinking
    Discussing
    Listing Ideas (preliminary outline)
    Gathering Information

          WRITING THE ROUGH DRAFT
    Reconsider preliminary outline, revise if desired.
    Write the rough draft, focusing on ideas, with little
        concern for spelling and mechanics.

          REWRITING AND FINISHING
    Read the draft aloud and make any desired changes in **what**
        is said or **how** it is said.
    Write a second draft, including those changes.
        Read it aloud again to see if any further changes need to be made.
    Check: Usage Spelling Capitalization Punctuation
        Write the final draft.

Helping Children Appreciate Writing

As pointed out in Chapter 3, children normally enjoy scribbling "stories" during their preschool years—providing they have observed their parents or older siblings writing. They enjoy "reading" these stories and want to learn to write so they can be like older members of their families. We can build on this appreciation of writing, in part, by responding to two questions in class discussions and through bulletin board displays.

Why did we invent writing? Information provided in Chapter 1 helped my students to understand why writing was invented. I also mentioned a few instances when I needed to write, such as making grocery lists and completing voter registration forms. The students often told about situations where they had to write, or when they had observed their parents writing. A list of different writing tasks was generated, then added to that list that I included in Chapter 1.

What has writing made possible? Understanding the importance that writing has played in the development of civilization is an important element when setting the

CHECKLIST FOR REWRITING MY ROUGH DRAFT

Focusing My Writing
_____Is it easy to tell who my audience is?

_____Are my reasons for writing apparent?

My Paragraphs
Have I started a new paragraph each time:

_____...a new main idea (what) is introduced?

_____...a new character (who) begins talking?

_____...a new place (where) is introduced?

_____...a new time (when) is introduced?

_____Is the main idea of each paragraph clear?

_____Have I told enough about each main idea?

_____Does each paragraph focus only on one main idea?

_____Does each sentence seem to lead to the next sentence?

_____Have I told about all of the main ideas?

_____Are my paragraphs (main ideas) in the best order?

_____Does each paragraph seem to lead to the next paragraph?

My Sentences
_____Does each sentence clearly say what I mean?

_____Do parts of the sentence agree in number?

_____Have I maintained the same point of view?

_____Have I used different sentence beginnings?

_____Have I avoided over-using words like _said, and so_, and _and then_?

_____Have I used different types of sentences?

_____Have I avoided using unnecessary words?

My Usage
Check uses of:

_____*their/they're/there*

_____*then/than*

_____*your/you're*

_____*was/were/where*

_____*to/too/two*

_____*no/know/now*

_____*it's/its*

_____*heard/herd*

_____*buy/by/bye*

_____*lose/loose*

continued on next page

Checklist for Rewriting continued

_____*our/hour*
_____*went/gone*
_____*run/ran*
_____*did/done*
_____*doesn't/don't*
_____*he/she/I*
_____*him/her/me*
_____*clothes/close*
_____*saw/seen*
_____*were/we're*
_____*took/taken*
_____*come/came*
_____*ran/run*
_____*rang/rung*
_____*there is/there are*

My Mechanics
_____Have I capitalized the first letter of each sentence and the first letter of all other important words?
_____Have I used the correct punctuation mark at the end of each sentence?
_____Have I used commas only where I paused briefly when reading my writing aloud?
_____Have I used apostrophe marks only where needed?
_____Have I used quotation marks to show the words spoken by someone?

My Handwriting
_____Is my handwriting neat, easy to read?

My Spelling
_____Have I spelled all words correcty?

Documentation
_____Have I included footnotes and entries in my bibliography to show where I got information from other sources?

stage for writing. Information provided in Chapter 1 also helped children to realize the historical significance of the invention of writing—how our body of knowledge greatly expanded and became increasingly complex as a result of writing. "Invention trees" were developed during class discussions to illustrate how inventions depended on previous developments and how writing made possible the accumulation of knowledge necessary for their invention. For example, the invention tree for the bicycle was designed as follows:

INVENTION TREE FOR THE BICYCLE

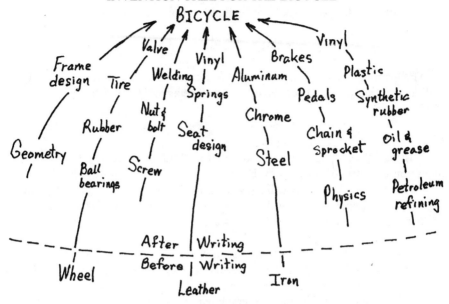

We can also facilitate children's appreciation of writing through other means, such as enjoying stories and poems from children's literature and stories written by us teachers. Realizing that their favorite movies are nearly always in book form first can also help children appreciate the importance of writing, as can visits to the local newspaper, printers, and publishers.

Some basic guidelines to remember are:

1. Writing experiences should focus on real interests and concerns of children as much as possible.
2. Provide opportunities for children to talk before writing.
3. Establish specific criteria for each type of material. Generated during class discussions before writing, these serve to guide students' efforts during writing.
4. Allow students to assist each other, such as reading aloud to their partners and proofreading each other's work.
5. Occasionally allow students to form pairs and write materials as a team.
6. Break the writing experience into steps, such as developing a preliminary outline, developing a story synopsis, and writing the rough draft, and monitor each child's progress, setting deadlines if necessary.
7. Be sure to allow enough time for students to finish their materials.
8. Provide opportunities for students to enjoy what they have written by reading their materials to each other and by publicizing their materials.
9. Avoid grading everything children write. It's also important for the teacher to be an audience and a facilitator.

10. The teacher should be a writer and share her writings with her students, including her rough drafts as well as her finished works.

Stimulating Writing Activities

The learning activities included in this section span a wide range of interests, abilities, and purposes. They have been well received by students at appropriate levels.

Directions

Writing directions appeals to a wide range of children, especially when they have opportunities to try to follow them. Each child chooses the purpose of his directions, then writes them. After he has finished writing his directions, a classmate tries—if appropriate at school—to follow the directions by doing **exactly** what they say. Some of the more popular directions may focus on:

> Making a peanut butter sandwich
> Going from my house to school
> Fixing a flat tire on a bicycle
> Drawing a pattern on graph paper
> Going from one place on campus to another place on campus
> Constructing a certain form with blocks, etc.
> Going from one place to another place on a roadmap

Follow-up discussions with my students for the purpose of identifying the criteria of good directions produced the following chart:

GOOD DIRECTIONS

1. Did I tell each important step?
2. Did I tell the steps in the right order?
3. Did I say exactly what I meant—*left* when I meant *left*, and so on?

When telling how to make something, also:

4. Did I include a list of ingredients and amounts?

When telling how to draw something, also:

5. Did I include directions for drawing lines?
6. Did I tell size and shape of each form?

When telling how to get from one place to another place, also:

7. Did I include numbers of highways, and the names of streets and other important features?
8. Did I tell the total distance, then distances between landmarks?

An adaptation of this activity allows the students to read a set of directions, then attempt to guess the purpose or identify the final destination.

Descriptions

The following activities promote the development of the ability to describe, an element common to many types of writing.

Describing a Peanut. This activity enhances the student's powers of observation and description. It begins with each student selecting a peanut (in the hull) from a pile of peanuts. He must then write a description of that peanut, including marks and other distinguishing features such as size, shape, or color. His peanut is then put back into the pile of peanuts. His classmates are then challenged to identify his peanut by reading his description and carefully examining the peanuts. Students take turns sharing their descriptions. A discussion then focuses on the characteristics of a good description. The following chart was generated with my middle school students and displayed for future reference.

CHARACTERISTICS OF A GOOD DESCRIPTION

1. Have I included all important details?
2. Have I described how it looks, sounds, feels, tastes, and smells?
3. Have I used exact words rather than words like *good, nice*, and *big*?
4. Have I included the shapes and sizes of the parts?
5. Have I told how the parts are arranged?
6. Have I compared it with things my reader already knows?

Whose Face? The student is directed to write a description of a classmate's face. He is told that his classmates will attempt to guess who the person is after he has finished his description and read it to them. He is reminded to use **exact** words rather than words like *pretty, nice*, and *ugly*, and focus on the following:

General shape of the face (round, oval, square, triangular)
Color and shape of the eyes, and whether they are wide-set or close-set
Shape, size, and other distinguishing features of the nose
Fullness and position of the cheeks
Size and shape of the chin (pointed, round, square)
Shape of the forehead (hairline)
Any other distingishing features, such as a scar or freckles

This activity may be adapted to that of a detective in charge of solving a case. The student pretends that he is a detective assigned to write a description of the person charged with the wrongdoing. A facial sketch might even be included.

Guess What (or Who, Where)? The student is allowed to select an object, then write a description of it. His classmates are then asked to identify the object after hearing his desciption. Students take turns sharing their descriptions. Caution: Be sure to remind the students not to give any hints about the *purpose* of the object.

Say What You Mean

One of the common problems children have when writing is saying what they mean. That is, their written messages sometimes don't communicate what is meant— for a variety of reasons. Sometimes something is omitted, the wrong word is used, or a word or phrase is misplaced. Whatever the cause, the result is sometimes embarrassing, sometimes humorous. The **Say What You Mean** bulletin board causes children to realize that adults have the same problem and that the result is often humorous. It also helps children deal with this problem in a nonthreatening, humorous way.

Say What You Mean Bulletin Board. This bulletin board serves as the basis of class discussions that focus on writing clearly and concisely. I usually titled it "Say What You Mean" or something like "Say What?" A misstatement, including its context, is displayed on the bulletin board. After the initial laugh, the students are asked what was so funny? The apparent discrepancy between what was written and what was meant is pointed out. The discussion then leads to what **should** have been written.

Where did I get these misstatements? From my college students, colleagues, and my own observations. One example is the following statement from a sign in a cafeteria: "Shoes are required to eat here." Someone had written below it,"Socks must eat elsewhere."

Other misstatements were drawn from a variety of sources, such as church bulletins, accident reports, and excuses for children's absenses from school. Then I learned that hundreds of these are conveniently available in one source: Richard Lederer's *Anguished English*.[1] I highly recommend his publication for this purpose. Below are a few of the many misstatements that my students enjoyed.

From traffic accident reports:[2]
> "The guy was all over the road. I had to swerve a number of times before I hit him."

> "In my attempt to kill a fly, I drove into a telephone pole."

From parents' excuses explaining their children's absences from school:[3]
> "Please excuse Mary from being absent. She was sick and I had her shot."

"Carlos was absent yesterday because he was playing football. He was hurt in the growing part."

From church bulletins:[4]

"For those of you who have children and don't know it, we have a nursery downstairs."

"This being Easter Sunday, we will ask Mrs. White to come forward and lay an egg on the altar."

"Remember in prayer the many who are sick of our church and community."

From classified ads:[5]

"Our experienced mom will care for your child. Fenced yard, meals, and smacks included."

Personal Experience Writing.

The Personal Experience Story. This is one of the most adaptable writing experiences of children, beginning with the dictated group experience story in kindergarten. It is equally suitable for seventh graders or seniors in high school because it is based on a meaningful first-hand experience of the writer. It is the easiest type of narrative material for students to write.

Students especially enjoy sharing this type of material. They are especially interested in stories written by their teacher that are based on her childhood experiences. One of my personal experience stories that my students enjoyed, "Flight of the Buzzard," is included in the Appendix.

Personal experience stories of beginning writers are typically written in first person and are usually told in a straight-forward, chronological manner. Gaps sometimes occur in the flow of these stories because children sometimes forget part of what they are writing about, or they think a part of the story without including it in their writing.

How did I help my middle school students write this type of material? First, I read one or two personal experience stories that had been written by students the previous year. I also mentioned that I would later share one of my own stories. I then introduced this writing experience as a process and suggested specific steps that would help them write their stories. Class discussions focused on different types of story beginnings in selected literary works, and I explained the difference between *first person* and *third person.* Two versions of my story, "Flight of the Buzzard," illustrated writing in the first person and writing in the third person. The following process was displayed on a chart in the classroom.

HOW TO WRITE A STORY

1. Choose an interesting or unusual experience to write about.

2. Outline or list the sequence of events, including the opening scene, events during the story, and closing scene.

3. Decide:
   ...if it is to be in first person or third person.
   ...whether or not to include dialogue.
   ...which type of story beginning to write.

4. Write a rough draft.

5. Read the story aloud and make any desired changes.

6. Read aloud again and, if necessary, revise the story again.

7. Proofread the story for the purpose of correcting any mistakes in spelling and mechanics.

8. Write the final version, including desired drawings or pictures and corrections in mechanics.

Criteria for this type of material were generated, then displayed on a chart similar to the one beginning on page 77.

Children tend to experience certain difficulties when writing personal experience stories. Writing dialogue that sounds real and is correctly punctuated and capitalized is a challenge. Inadequate description is also a common shortcoming. They sometimes use certain sentence beginnings over and over, such as "And so..." and "And then...." Beginning paragraphs in the right places, usage, spelling, and mechanical errors, especially overuse of the comma, are also problems. Proofreading practice and examination of stories in their readers help children overcome these difficulties. Overuse of *said* in dialogue can be remedied by helping children identify other words that are more descriptive. A list of words that my students generated was displayed on a chart similar to the one beginning on page 78.

My Scar. The scar story is appropriate for nearly all children since most of them have at least one scar. It rests on the premise that behind each scar is a story waiting to be told. Before writing, discuss what might be included in the story. Items often included are the setting, what the scar looks like, where it is located, how it happened, the funny part about my scar, the treatment that I received, how my parents reacted to my injury, and how I could have prevented the injury that resulted in the scar.

INGREDIENTS OF A GOOD PERSONAL EXPERIENCE STORY

Story Content

1. Have I chosen an unusual or especially enjoyable experience that my classmates will be interested in?

2. Have I begun my story in an interesting way?
   ...a description of a character
   ...a description of the setting
   ...a conversation between characters
   ...a statement that identifies the basic nature of the experience ("I thought no one would remember my birthday. Was I in for a surprise.")
   ...a short description of the background related to the experience ("I had been saving money to buy the model airplane for three months.")

3. Have I included enough details so my reader will "see a movie" in his mind as he reads?

Too General	*Better*
It was a nice day.	In the clear, blue sky the sun shone brightly. It felt warm on my back as I ....
Aunt Mary was angry.	Aunt Mary fowned, then turned and walked briskly toward the ....
It was an old house.	Only traces of faded yellow paint remained. Window screens were rusted away, and one of the two remaining shutters hung precariously by one hinge.

4. Have I included enough clues about the main character(s)?

5. Does the dialogue sound real? Does it help reveal my characters' feelings?

6. Does my ending finish the story or hint at a future problem rather than just summarize the story?

Summary	*Better*
We had lots of fun.	Nicole smiled and said, "....

Mechanical Considerations

7. Is my story written neatly?

continued on next page

continued from page 77

8. Have I used standard forms except where nonstandard usage is important in my story?

9. Have I correctly capitalized and punctuated my sentences?

10. Have I started a new paragraph each time:
    ...a new main idea (WHAT) is introduced?
    ...a new character (WHO) begins talking?
    ...a new place (WHERE) is introduced?
    ...a new time (WHEN) is introduced?

11. Have I avoided run-on sentences and sentence fragments except where they are important in my story?

12. Have I spelled words correctly?

SUBSTITUTES FOR "SAID"

When Characters Are Talking

added	griped	retorted
advised	groaned	roared
agreed	growled	screamed
announced	grumbled	shouted
answered	guessed	shrieked
asked	hollered	snarled
barked	howled	sobbed
bawled	inquired	stammered
beamed	interrupted	stuttered
beckoned	jested	suggested
begged	laughed	threatened
called	moaned	thundered
commanded	muttered	vowed
complained	ordered	whimpered
coughed	pleaded	whined
cried	questioned	whispered
cringed	remarked	yelled
demanded	remembered	yelped
exclaimed	replied	
explained	requested	
gasped	responded	
giggled		

When Characters Are Thinking

thought	remembered	wondered

The Autobiography. This is, of course, a type of personal experience story. It is potentially a more lengthy writing experience, especially for older students. The student, however, may focus on a particular period of his life rather than try to write a story about his entire life. It is usually a more meaningful writing experience when the student focuses on special events and people and tells how they influenced or shaped his life. The student should feel free to write about unpleasant experiences, such as divorce and death, and express his feelings about these events. Otherwise, the autobiography may be just a series of major events presented in chronological order—with few details and little meaning.

Story Titles. Sometimes titles help students think of a personal experience to write about. Some that students have responded favorably to include:

When I Got Real Mad
When My Mom/Dad Got Real Mad At Me
The Scariest Experience Of My Life
The Noise At My Window
My Dad's/Mom's Driving
How To Raise A Dog/Cat
Putting Up With My Older Brother/Sister
Putting Up With My Little Brother/Sister
My Favorite Season/Holiday
How My Life Will Be When I'm 30 Years Old
If I Could Be Invisible For A Day
How I'm Gonna Raise My Kids
If I Could Be The School Principal For A Day
My Best Friend
If I Won $1000
A Day In The Life Of My Shoe
The Disadvantage Of Being (8) Years Old
The Time When I Felt Very Sad
The Day When Everybody Treated Me Like A Weed
My Favorite Grandparent/Cousin/Uncle/Aunt
My Biggest Gripe
My Parents Were Very Proud Of Me
When I Did Something Really Dumb
How To Avoid Being Grounded
My Favorite Pastime

The Time Machine. The student is given a decorated box that is identified as a time machine. It has two buttons on it. Directions are: Push one button to go forward in your life. Push the other button to go backward in your life. Tell which button you would push, why you choose that button, and how your life would be different.

The Hands Story. The student outlines his right hand on paper several times, then cuts the outlined hands out and staples them together at the thumb. On the first, he writes a title like "My Hands Do Many Things." On each following hand he writes something his hands do.

The Face a Mother Loves. The student is given a closeup picture of an orangutan with the following caption: This is the face a mother dearly loves. What are some of the things your mother/father loves about you? How do you know this? What do you like about yourself? Is there anything you would change?

Imaginative Narrative Writing

The Imaginative Story. Some refer to this type of writing as "creative" writing because most of the events, characters, and plot exist only in the writers's imagination. It may, however, be based to some extent on some real direct or indirect experience. Whatever the label, this type of writing is an adaptable writing experience. Children begin writing these stories at the primary level and continue writing them as they proceed up through the grades.

Although the personal experience story and the creative story share many elements, the creative story is much more challenging to write because it requires the writer to create a problem and plot rather than merely tell about one of his experiences. The degree of originality, however, may range from stories that are completely original to those that are merely different versions of popular stories, such as a rewrite of the "The Three Billy Goats Gruff" from the viewpoint of the troll.

When my students were ready to begin writing their stories, the charts displayed earlier for writing personal experience stories were helpful. However, another chart listing the characteristics of a creative story was also helpful. The chart appears on page 81.

The process for writing an imaginative story is basically the same as that used for the personal experience story. The writer may write a story synopsis first, or either outline/list the events of the story prior to writing or develop a story blueprint as illustrated in the form on page 82.

As with the personal experience story, students will display unusual interest in original stories written by their teacher. Reading a story written by their teacher is an excellent way of stimulating children to write their own stories. It is, however, very important that the teacher also makes available her rough draft and subsequent revisions. The story problem and plot should, like the writing style, be on a level appropriate for the students. Criteria for judging the personal experience story can easily be modified to accommodate this type of material.

The Paper Bag Story. A child or pair of children is given a paper bag containing several familiar objects. Their task is to create a story, including all (or some) of the objects in the bag. They are allowed to build the objects into their story in whatever manner they choose.

INGREDIENTS OF AN ORIGINAL STORY

1. **A plot**, including a problem or puzzling situation to be overcome, and:
   ...events that introduce the problem or its possibility.
   ...events that complicate the problem.
   ...events that solve the problem (if it is solved).

2. **Details**: Include enough so the reader will be able to "see a movie" in his mind as he reads.

3. **Characters** that seem real.

4. **Drama**: Events during the story that build excitement and keep the reader's interest.

5. **Setting(s)**: Times and places that fit the action.

6. **Dialogue**: Conversation and thoughts of characters that help carry the flow of the story.

Envelope Story. The student selects an envelope containing picures of different places, such as a beach, an old house, etc. She then chooses one of the pictures as the setting for her story. An alternative is to require the student to use all of the pictures in the story.

The Bagel Burger. The student is given a bagel and the following instructions: A famous hamburger chain (name one) has asked you to create its new bagel burger. Here is the bagel. What will you put on it? What will your advertising jingle sound like?

The Tall Tale. The student is reminded about some popular tall tales, such as Pecos Bill, then challenged to create a tall tale of his own. He is encouraged to let her imagination "really go free."

Sentence Combining

Students also seem to enjoy rewriting teacher-written materials that challenge them to combine sentences. This sometimes becomes a contest to see who can rewrite the material with the fewest sentences. This practice should, of course, occur only **after** students have demonstrated that they can write clear simple sentences, and after they have been shown different ways to combine sentences. Students should also practice combining pairs of sentences before they are challenged to rewrite paragraphs.

Different ways of combining sentences should be introduced in the following order.

Bill and Mary went home.

BLUEPRINT FOR AN ORIGINAL STORY

Author: _____

What the story is about:
_____

_____

_____

Characters: _____

_____

_____

Story told in (check): ___1st person   ____3rd person

Directions: In the first bubble, briefly tell how your story begins. Now, finish your blueprint, including one **main** event in each bubble. Include just enough in each bubble to guide you later when you write your story. Limit your blueprint to not more than 6 or 7 bubbles.

Sergio *builds and sells* model airplanes.
Michelle went swimming, *and* Allison went shopping.
I wanted to go fishing, *but* Mom said that I had to mow the lawn.
She's going to Disneyland next summer, *or* she's going to visit her aunt in Oregon.
The book *on the shelf* is mine.
Cinnamon is a spice *that* is grown in the tropics.
The girl *who lives next door* is my cousin.
My first grade teacher, *Miss Hansen*, was my favorite teacher.
After I got home, I ate lunch.
She wasn't there *when he got home*.

A final precaution: These different ways of combining sentences should be introduced one at a time, beginning in the primary grades, and not be completed until at least the sixth or seventh grade.

The following is an example that I provided for my seventh graders.

I am going on vacation. My mom is going. My dad is going. It will be in June. We will go to Wyoming. We will spend two weeks on a ranch. It is a large ranch. It is a working ranch. The owner raises cattle. We will help with the chores. We will drive cattle. We will brand cattle.

Fluency Writing

This activity requires students to write spontaneously for a few minutes. (The time period is lengthened with experience.) Students are required to write continuously during this period without stopping. That is, their writing instruments must move constantly. They are provided with a sentence or the beginning of the sentence as a starter. They must copy the prompt and, on cue, continue the story. They are told not to worry about spelling or mechanical errors—just focus on keeping the story going until they are told to stop. After they stop writing, the stories are read aloud by class volunteers or read anonymously by the teacher.

Students quickly realize that they can keep their pens moving, and that they can write quickly. They are frequently surprised and amused at the diversity and creativeness of their classmates. This activity, then, helps build student confidence. It helps convince them that they **can** write! Writer's block? It becomes less of a problem.

Some prompts that my middle school students responded to well were:

"When I got home, Mom said there was a letter for me in the mail."

"During my English class, a student aide came to the door and handed Mr. Hicks a note—which he then gave to me."

"When I got up this morning and started to put toothpaste on my toothbrush ...."

"I opened the refrigerator to get milk for breakfast and ...."

"Just as I started to bite into my hamburger ...."

"As I stepped into my bedroom, I felt a strange presence."

"It was midnight when I was suddenly awakened by a scraping sound at my window."

"As I walked downstairs to the basement, ..."

The Letter

Students usually enjoy writing letters to relatives or important public figures as a class assignment. The teacher should have envelopes and stamps on hand in class, and plan to mail the letters. Addresses of popular singing groups and movie stars are periodically published in various magazines for teens.

Dear Mr. President. Writing letters to the President of the United States or to his office for information is a captivating idea for most children—especially when they know they will receive a response from him. When should these letters be written? Whenever a major national or international event occurs that is of concern to the children, or when they want a special greeting sent to someone special. One special service provided by the White House is the birthday greetings from the President of the United States to anyone over 70 years of age, or a congratulatory note sent to any couple celebrating a wedding anniversary of 50 years or more. The address of the President of the United States (and other public officials) is usually published in the telephone directory and at the local post office. For the birthday greetings or the anniversary note, write to the address below.

> The White House Greetings Office
> 1600 Pennsylvania Avenue
> Washington, D.C. 20500

Dear Abby. This activity consists of providing students with letters written to Dear Abby and, without revealing Abby's responses, writing replies to the letters. Student replies are then read and discussed, then compared with Abby's reply. (The "Dear Gabby" column in our school newspaper responded to student letters about various concerns.)

Proofreading Practice

Students enjoy proofreading letters and other teacher-prepared materials, especially when it's not for a grade. I provided a copy of prepared material for each student to examine on his own or with a partner. We then examined it together when I displayed it with the overhead projector. Teams can also be formed and students can compete to "see who can find the most errors." Below is an example of one of the letters that I provided for my middle school students.

July 17, 1992
140 Green Streat
Las Cruces, NM 88001

The Dinosaur Hamburger
753 Allen Street
Las Cruces, NM 88001

Dear sir:

   My daughter will be having her forth birthday on July 28.
I understand you provide partys for children. Will you be
able to set one up for my child on that day. I would also like
to no how much you charge, how many childrn you can acommodate
and when it could be scheduled? Please let me no what would
be bes.

Sincerly yours

Mary Allison Jones

P.S. I realy think she will like this partie.

Filling Out Forms

   To adults, filling out forms is certainly not a pleasant task. But reality demands, as demonstrated in Chapter 1, that we fill out forms for a wide range of purposes. Apparently, considerable attention should be focused on this task. Attention should also be given to developing forms.

   How can we cause children to enjoy practicing filling out forms? The answer is to select the **right** forms! What are they **interested** in? What would they **like** to do? Some that children often respond to favorably are listed below.

     Application for employment at a popular hamburger chain
     Application for a job as a lifeguard
     Application for a driver's license
     Application for auto insurance
     Warranty card for a stereo
     Registration for contests (of all sorts)
     Subscription forms for popular magazines
     Development of a resume'
     Contract to purchase a motorcycle, car

Form for an airline ticket
Application for a loan to purchase a motor vehicle
Renter's contract
Marriage license
Voter registration (for school elections)
Application for various student jobs at school
Application for membership in various youth organizations
Registration as a candidate for student council
Application to enter show animal at fair
Application for social security number

When do we begin instruction in completing forms? Although learning to complete simple forms, such as the library card, might begin quite early in school, most instruction does not need to begin until the upper elementary grades. We shouldn't, however, underestimate children's readiness to begin practicing this skill. Fifth and sixth graders do respond favorably to most of those forms listed above. Just listen to them howl when they must choose a classmate as a spouse and "apply" for a marriage license.

News Writing

The News Story. Writing news stories offers children a different kind of writing experience. While most of their writing is rather personal and subjective, the news story stresses facts, is objective, and is written in the *third person*. Probably the most difficult task for children is to make the transition to the third person. These elements make this type of writing unsuitable for the primary grades. It is taught more easily to middle school students. The transition from the personal experience story written in the first person to the news story, however, is facilitated by rewriting personal experience stories as news stories.

How did I help my students understand the nature of the news story? We examined newspapers and a model story that I had written as a means of discovering the characteristics unique to this type of writing. My news story was based on a personal experience and was displayed via the overhead projector. The news story appears on page 87.

Byline and **dateline** were introduced, and the **pyramid** writing style was examined. After the basic nature of headlines was noted, students practiced rewriting sentences into headlines, and choosing the best headline for a given article. After illustrating the differences between *first person*, *second person*, and *third person*, person were explained, we practiced rewriting stories in the third person. Discussions also clarified the criteria for news stories—which were then displayed on a chart in the classroom. The chart is shown on page 87.

News stories can be included in the class newspaper; or, if no newspaper is being produced, stories can be displayed on the bulletin board. A news story that my students seemed to enjoy is presented on page 88.

PILOT SURVIVES SCARE

By Jerral Hicks.

Fort Collins, Colorado. While making his second solo flight in an ultralight airplane yesterday, Jerral Hicks made one error. He ran out of gas. When asked how it happened, Hicks said, "I guess I just got carried away. I was concentrating on my techniques so hard that I forgot to watch my gas tank."

Hicks had been practicing approaches and landings for about an hour. Then it happened—at 400 feet up! The engine quit while he was headed away from the landing field. "I never knew quiet could be so quiet," he said. "I nearly panicked, thinking I was going to crash into the corn field below. Then I remembered how my instructor had showed me to land with the engine off." Hicks said he pushed forward on the stick so he wouldn't stall, then turned back toward the field. "My heart was pounding, but I just kept thinking about what I **had** to do."

Fortunately, Hicks had enough altitude to reach the field. He said the landing was a fast one, but the smoothest of the day. He plans to check his fuel tank more often during future flights. Hicks highly recommends a flight training program to those who want to fly an ultralight airplane.

CHECKLIST FOR NEWS STORIES

My Headline:
Is it short and attention-getting?
Does it include a **doing** word and one or more **naming** words?

My Byline:
Is it next to the left margin?
Is it moved down two spaces below the headline?

My Dateline:
Is it located a space below the byline?
Is it next to the left margin?

My Story:
*Does my story begin on the same line and immediately follow the dateline?
*Does my first sentence clearly tell the main idea of the story, perhaps by expanding the headline into a sentence?
*Does each following sentence tell some fact about the story? (Who? What? When? Where? Why? How?)
*Do I first identify each person by his whole name, then refer to him by his last name or a third person pronoun?
*Do I use first person pronouns only in quotes?
*Except in quotes and sentences telling about the future, are most verbs in the past tense?

CHICKEN WHIPS ACEVEDO

By Peter Barron.

Peter Barron's Chicken House. Yesterday, while visiting Peter Barron, Lino Acevedo, 13, was attacked by a killer chicken. When asked how it happened, Acevedo said, "I was blind-sided. I never saw the chicken coming." He quickly added, "But I don't want a rematch!"

Barron asked Acevedo if he would like to see the game chickens his father was raising. After viewing the chickens in a large pen for a moment, Barron told Acevedo that he could step into the pen and pet one if he wanted to. Barron opened the door but remained outside the pen as Acevedo stepped inside.

Suddenly, dirt began flying everywhere. Acevedo started jumping and yelling for Barron to open the door. The chicken was in hot pursuit.

Finally, Acevedo crouched down and covered his head with his hands and arms. Barron, laughing loudly, then opened the door and rescued Acevedo. Acevedo claimed that he could have whipped the chicken, but he didn't want to hurt it.

Printed by permission.

Headlines. The student selects a headline from a group of headlines and writes a story that fits the headline. Watch for the unexpected! (This should follow instruction about writing news stories.)

The Editorial. Children begin arguing at an early age, perhaps over a toy in the sandbox. Arguments continue as they enter school, and they discover that others don't always see things as they do. They also recognize that they don't always agree with their parents.

Why include the editorial in the writing program? It capitalizes on this natural element in relationships. That is, it focuses on the fact that people normally disagree about many things in life. This is particularly true in our society since it is grounded in a democratic philosophy in which examination of issues is a cornerstone. Inclusion of editorializing in the writing program is a natural extension of the debate in the oral language program. It helps children learn a constructive way of dealing with differences of opinion. It is also a response to the need to help individuals examine and explain their own beliefs in a thoughtful, effective manner. In addition, it should help children learn to respect the opinions of others, no matter how different those opinions may be. Children should learn that the editorial is a thoughtful statement or argument for or against something. Its purpose is to influence the reader's opinion about an issue or cause the reader to do something the writer desires.

After examining sample editorials in class, the chart on page 89 was displayed in the classroom for reference.

Writing the Editorial

Editorials usually include:
1. A statement that clearly identifies the issue (or problem)
2. A statement for or against that issue
3. Reasons, with supporting facts for each, such as statistics and examples, including references to *who, what, when, when,* and *where*
4. A suggested solution to the issue or problem, or a way of avoiding a possible problem

Editorials do not include:
1. Name-calling
2. Generalizations like "Everybody believes ...," and "Nobody likes ..."
3. Vague terms such as *good, nice, bad, sort of,* and *wonderful*

Listening to children during opening discussions about things that make them angry or things that they don't like will help identify issues or problems that are appropriate for a class. Those that seemed to stir considerable student interest in my classes and other classes were:

*Which makes a better pet—a cat or a dog?

*Should skateboards be banned?

*Should bicycle riders be **required** to wear helmets?

*Should people be **required** to wear seatbelts in cars?

*Should students be allowed to participate in athletics when they are not passing?

*Should teachers be allowed to smoke on campus?

*Should deer hunting be banned?

*Should people be allowed to own guns?

*Which is best—living in the city, suburbs, or country?

*Should boxing be banned?

*People should not be allowed to get their driver's licenses until they are 18 years old!

*Students should not be required to attend school after they are 14 years old.

*Should sex education be included in the school curriculum?

*Should the death penalty be banned?

*Should people be allowed to own pit bulldogs?

*Students should be allowed to dress the way they want for school.

*Should alcoholic beverages be prohibited?

*Should smoking be permitted in public places?

*What should we do about drugs in school?

More descriptive editorial topics are also effective. Two that my students responded favorably to were:

*You've been selected as the outstanding student who is to make a speech at the PTA. Your topic is: How Parents Can Help Their Children Do Well In School.

Write your speech, telling what you intend to tell the parents.

*You've been appointed as a student representative on the school board. What changes in the school are you going to recommend to the board? How will you justify these changes?

Class Newspaper or Magazine. Writing, producing, and distributing a class newspaper or magazine is a major undertaking that requires considerable time. How, then, can the production of either be justified? First, it provides students with meaningful writing experiences. It also provides opportunities for them to develop skills in management since they must work together and meet deadlines. It may also provide opportunities for students to develop skills in advertising if ads are included. Finally, it they may provide experiences in sales and distribution if it is sold.

Children initially respond very favorably to the idea of a class newspaper or magazine, but may lose interest if they undertake such a project with an unrealistic picure of the amount of work required. Therefore, we should be realistic with them when discussing the feasibility of producing either of these materials. If students make an informed decision to produce a newspaper or magazine, they will be more likely to sustain the necessary effort.

What does production of a class newspaper or magazine entail? It requires decisions about what to include, selection of the management staff, making specific job assignments, and setting deadlines for writers, photographers, proofreaders, typists, copiers, and distributors. An **Activity Management Sheet** should be displayed to help students remember who is responsible for each task and when each task is supposed to be completed.

How often might the newspaper or magazine be published? Depending on the content, how much class time is available, and the age of the students, it might be published on a weekly basis, but it is more realistic to publish on a bi-weekly or even monthly basis.

Plays

Writing plays is an enjoyable experience for children, especially if they are allowed to perform the plays with their classmates. The first attempts to write plays should focus on converting children's personal experience stories to scripts. This is even easier when the stories already include dialogue. I demonstrated how to do this by rewriting one of my personal experience stories, "Flight of the Buzzard," as a play. To convert a story to a play, children realized that they needed to (a) change the format, (b) convert the story to dialogue, and (c) add scene and costume descriptions.

Poetry

This type of material can be a source of much enjoyment to children if certain practices are avoided. How can we turn children off to poetry? The following practices usually contribute to a negative attitude toward poetry.

Require children to memorize poems and recite them in front of the class.
Always grade their recitations of poems.
Require all the students to memorize and recite the same poem.
Don't allow children to share their favorite poems.
Expect children to write poems without first enjoying some of their favorite
poems.
Expect children to write poems without first studying rhyming patterns and poetic
forms.

These practices are particularly threatening to students who have yet to conquer their
stage fright. If a child *wants* to recite a favorite poem in front of her class, fine. But
don't require her to do so!

Children seem to enjoy reading orally their favorite poems, often those that are
silly. My sixth graders and seventh graders thoroughly enjoyed rereading poems in
Silverstein's *Where the Sidewalk Ends*,[6] and hearing me read selected poems from
Arbuthnot's *Time for Poetry*.[7] (I say "rereading" because they had enjoyed reading
the poems in earlier grades.) This helps children to appreciate poetry, including the
silly, serious, even sad. Reading familiar poems aloud also helps children develop
stage presence. During these readings, various forms and patterns, such as the
couplet, triplet, quatrain, haiku, and the limerick, can be pointed out. These can be
reinforced through additional poems on transparencies.

Basic forms that need to be taught include:

Couplet: two lines that rhyme
Triplet: three lines that rhyme
Quatrain: four line poem with one of the following patterns:
             aabb, abab, abcb

Students should be shown examples that illustrate how the above patterns can be
extended into multiple verse poems. These examples should also illustrate how
different verses in a multiple verse poem can follow different rhyming patterns.

Other types of poems are also sources of enjoyment to children. Most notably,
they are:

Haiku: A three line poem consisting of five syllables in the first
            line, seven in the second line, and five in the third line.
            It usually focuses on some aspect of nature and expresses
            a rather somber, gentle mood. It contains no rhyming
Tanaka: Similar to the haiku, except that a fourth line and a fifth
            line are added, each consisting of seven syllables.
Limerick: A five line poem that is humorous or silly. It always follows
            the same rhyming pattern: aabba. The third line is shorter than the
            other lines.

Poems can be written so they display various graphic forms that are related to the
content of each poem. For example, a poem about a snake might be written in a
circular or coiled fashion. A poem about a dog might be written inside the outlined

form of a dog, even including a string of words for a tail. A poem about rain might be written inside the outline of a raindrop. A Halloween poem about a ghost might be written inside the outline of a ghost.

Three poems written by my students and me are:

FIRST FLOWER
by Jerral Hicks
Frail, short and shivering,
Trying to grow;
Leaning in the wind quivering,
Chilled by melting snow.

Bent and shriveled by light frost,
Will it die, all be lost?
Warm sun, blue sky above,
The first of spring's warm love.

WHAT WE CALL HALLOWEEN
by Becky Houghton
Ghosts and gobblins
And apples a bobbin'
Is what I'm talking about.

Tricks and treats
And spooky feats
And werewolves bein' so rout.

Vampires a roamin'
And witches a groanin'
And things that haven't been seen;
All have a weird party
Where none look very hearty
And we call it Halloween!

Printed by permission.

THAT LITTLE OLE CHIGGER
by anonymous sixth graders

That little ole chigger is quite a pest.
Grass is its nest.
The chigger has an ugly figure;
Into my skin he is quite a digger.
That ole chigger, he hides in the grass;
He'll hop on me and never even ask!

Once children begin writing their own poems, encourage them to share them with their classmates. With their permission, also publish their poems by displaying them on bulletin boards, encouraging the students to read them at PTA meetings, printing them in the school or local newspaper, and printing and binding them as books for the school library. The kids will love it!

NOTES

1. Richard Lederer, Anguished English, 1987 Reprint, (New York, NY: Dell Publishing, 1989.)

2. Lederer, 39-40.

3. Lederer, 23.

4. Lederer, 47-48.

5. Lederer, 57.

6. Shel Silverstein, Where the Sidewalk Ends (New York, NY: Harper Collins Publishers, 1974).

7. May Hill Arbuthnot and Shelton L. Root, Jr., Time for Poetry, 3rd ed. (Glenview, IL: Scott Foresman and Co., 1968).

CHAPTER 6: A WRITING CURRICULUM

Decisions about **what** to teach in writing have traditionally been based largely upon practical considerations, as well they should be. Concern has focused on writing needs for daily living and in the business world, including consideration for expressive, informative, persuasive, and literary needs.
The following questions provide direction for determining the writing curriculum.

What purposes of writing should be given attention in a writing curriculum for the elementary school?

What types of written materials will society likely expect this child to produce during his lifetime?

What rhetorical modes will children need to write?

What concepts and skills are inherent in the production of those materials?

What hierarchy of basic writing skills should be included in a writing curriculum for the elementary school?

How should the writing skills for the elementary school be sequenced?

How should learner attitude be considered in the writing program?

Purpose of Writing

Writing, because of its inconvenience, is the mode of communication that should most likely be associated with a clear purpose. How so? We avoid writing because of the time and mental concentration it requires, often choosing, instead, to just pick up the phone or waiting until we see "them" next time. When we **must** write, then, there is often a good reason for having to do so. Sometimes the reason is very obvious in our material; other times it is less apparent because of a lack of clarity or direction in the writing. Whatever the case, we use language for a variety of purposes, and writing is one channel through which we can achieve those purposes. Purposes for which we write include:

To inform	To inquire
To request	To entertain others
To entertain oneself	To console or comfort
To control others	To question
To persuade	To satisfy a need for achievement

Incumbent in effective writing is the need to establish a clear purpose for doing so. This is true for all writers. Simply put, clarity of purpose promotes clarity in writing! Unfortunately, we all too often encounter writing that seems unorganized, seems to lack a sense of direction or purpose. We try to understand, but wonder. This can be caused, in part, by a failure to establish a clear purpose **before** writing. For the beginning writer, a clear sense of purpose is especially helpful. It is important, then, that prior to writing, teachers should first focus their students' attention on the **purpose** for writing .

Types of Written Materials

As we write for different purposes, we necessarily produce different types of materials. What types of materials do we write? Examination of lists of writing experiences by college students provides considerable direction regarding the types of materials students need to learn to write. Consideration of materials written by other adults and children also provides useful information about what to include in the curriculum. A comprehensive list of those materials includes:

1. Titles and headlines
2. Social letters and notes, including get well notes, thank you notes, invitations, and notes of sympathy/condolences
3. Business letters for different purposes
4. Reports on research topics
5. Reports on scientific research
6. Announcements and notices
7. Directions that tell how to do something
8. Directions that tell how to make something

9. Directions that tell how to get from one place to another place
10. Personal experience stories
11. Created stories, plays, poetry
12. News stories
13. Summaries and reviews of books, films, and magazine articles
14. Advertisements
15. Editorials
16. Forms of many different types
17. Diaries
18. Journals
19. Logs of scientific data
20. Taking notes from printed sources
21. Taking notes from live sources
22. Topic outlines (word, phrase)

Rhetorical Modes

As pointed out in Chapter 2, four basic rhetorical modes, **description**, **narration**, **exposition**, and **persuasion**, are inherent in our writing. They are often used in various combinations in a given material. The writing curriculum, then, should provide for conceptual development and periodic direct instruction on an as-needed basis. Conceptual development should focus on those attributes appropriate for each as described in Chapter 2.

Although these modes are not always taught in isolation, the teacher needs to be alert to pupil abilities to produce them. Improvement of ability to produce them will be directly reflected in written materials. When combined with knowledge of children's interests and needs in skill development, the teacher will be better equipped to make decisions about future writing experiences.

Basic Concepts and Skills

Regardless of the type of material to be written, certain concepts and skills, such as spelling and legible handwriting, are essential to effective writing. Some concepts related to writing are:

To write
Pencil (pen, felt tip marker)
Keyboard
Left-to-right
Top-to-bottom
Letter
Capital letter
Lower case letter
Numeral

Line
Word
Sentence
Sentence that tells (declarative)
Sentence that asks (interrogative)
Sentence that expresses strong feeling (exclamatory)
Sentence that gives a command (imperative)
Simple sentence
Compound sentence
Complex sentence
Compound-complex sentence
Subject
Compound subject
Predicate
Compound predicate
Noun
Pronoun
Adjective
Verb
Adverb
Conjunction
Preposition
Phrase
Clause
Independent clause
Dependent clause
Punctuation
Period
Comma
Question mark
Exclamation mark
Colon
Semicolon
Hyphen
Paragraph
Topic sentence
Outline
Alphabetical order
Chronological order
List
To spell
Syllable
Vowel

Consonant
Homonym
Manuscript writing
Cursive writing
Some of the skills related to writing are:
Manipulating a writing instrument
Writing legibly
Operating a keyboard
Spelling words
Constructing sentences
Capitalizing words in sentences/titles/outlines/lists
Punctuating sentences/titles/outlines/lists
Constructing paragraphs
Sequencing paragraphs
Outlining various materials

Effectiveness in applying these skills affects not only the impact of the material upon the reader, but also the reader's opinion of the writer. It is important, then, that adequate attention be given to concept formations and skills that are critical to effective writing. They are organized in the skills chart beginning on page 100.

Sequence of Curriculum

Typically, a curriculum guide includes a scope and sequence chart that describes the contents and organization of the program. The chart includes statements that describe the goals and objectives that students are expected to achieve, and the concepts and skills they are to develop. These are then organized into a logical sequence that specifies what the learner is to encounter as he proceeds through the program—level by level. The scope and sequence chart, then, not only describes the content, but also indicates **when** various elements are to be introduced, then reviewed.

The chart is usually organized according to skill areas, such as punctuation or sentence sense. For example, a chart focusing on punctuation might indicate that uses of the period to be introduced in the first grade include (1) at the end of a sentence that tells and (2) after each number in a list. A chart delineating capitalization skills to be introduced in the first grade might include (1) the first word of a sentence, (2) the word *I*, (3) a person's first and last names, (4) the name of a school, town, and street, and (5) the day of the month.

Decisions regarding placement of specific concepts and skills in a program are supposedly based, in part, on children's normative development. Specific content, it is claimed, is introduced when children "are ready." It is based on the child's mental development and physical development, as well as the logical placement of that content in the subject matter.

CHART OF BASIC WRITING SKILLS

Note: This chart is comprised of those skill areas that are essential to the production of those different types of materials listed earlier. It does not include any of those materials themselves since they may be introduced at different times, depending upon a number of factors.

Sentence Sense

*The ability to write a group of related words that contains a subject and a predicate, has word order, and clearly and concisely says what the writer means
*The ability to generate sentences for different purposes
*The ability to write different sentence structures (simple, compound, complex, compound-complex)
*The ability to write sentences containing compound subjects and compound predicates

Persistent common problems needing special attention:
*Writing run-on sentences
*Writing sentence fragments
*Not writing what they mean because of incorrect word choice or word order, word omission, unclear referent, or general confusion
*Including unnecessary words
*No combining ideas (writing only simple sentences)

Paragraph Sense

*The ability to write a group of related sentences that focuses on one main idea, has effective order, and correct form
*The ability to vary sentence beginnings, lengths, and structures in paragraphs
*The ability to produce different paragraph patterns by locating topic sentences in different places
*The ability to organize related paragraphs in the most effective sequence
*The ability to write effective paragraphs for informative, expressive, persuasive, and literary purposes

Persistent common problems needing special attention:
*Writing paragraphs that do not have clear main ideas
*Not staying on the topic
*Writing sentences in the wrong sequence
*Not beginning a new paragraph when needed
*Beginning a new paragraph in the wrong place
*Not including enough information
*Not maintaining point of view
*Beginning sentences the same way in a paragraph, especially with *and so* and *and then.*
*Using only simple sentences
*Overuse of *said* to introduce quotations

Punctuation

*The ability to punctuate sentences correctly, inserting periods, question marks, commas, colons, hyphens, and quotation marks as appropriate
*The ability to insert appropriate punctuation marks in lists, titles, and outlines
*The ability to punctuate addresses, greetings, and salutations correctly
*The ability to punctuate poetic lines appropriately

continued on next page

*The ability to insert appropriate punctuation marks in footnotes and bibliographic entries

Persistent common problems needing special attention:
*Omitting end punctuation
*Placing a period at the end of each line on a page when it is inappropriate
*Placing a period at the end of a sentence that asks a question or that expresses strong feeling
*Omitting the comma between independent clauses that are joined by *and, or,* or *but.*
*Omitting apostrophes in possessive nouns
*Inserting unneeded commas
*Using quotation marks incorrectly
*Omitting commas in a series of three or more items in a sentence
*Omitting a comma after an introductory phrase of five or more words in a sentence
*Omitting commas to set off quotations in a sentence

Capitalization
*The ability to begin the first word and all other important words in sentences with a capital letter
*The ability to begin each important word in a title with a capital letter
*The ability to capitalize appropriate words in addresses
*The ability to capitalize appropriate words in greetings and salutations
*The ability to capitalize appropriate words in outlines/lists/titles, and other forms

Persistent common problems needing special attention:
*Omitting capital letter in the second word of a compound proper noun (i.e., Mississippi River)
*Not capitalizing the pronoun *I*
*Not capitalizing the name of a language or nationality
*Confusion about when to capitalize *mother, father*
*Not capitalizng appropriate words in an address
*Not capitalizing appropriate words in a title

Spelling
*The ability to spell words correctly in sentences/lists/and all other formats

Persistent common problems needing special attention:
*Confusion of homonyms
*Spelling non-phonetic words phonetically
*Omitting silent letters
*Incorrect formation of plurals
*Transposing letters
*Inserting unnecessary letters
*Failing to double the final consonant when needed in derivatives
*Not changing the *y* to *i* when needed in derivatives
*Confusion about when to drop the final *e* when forming derivatives

continued on next page

As noted above, the primary goal of the spelling program is to teach children to **spell** words. Commercially-available spelling programs typically emphasize vocabulary development, the learning of new words. However, vocabulary development, I believe, is **not** a legitimate goal of the spelling program in the elementary school. Why? Because the spelling program should focus on words that children and adults actually include in their everyday writing. And which words do we write? Those that are already in our speaking vocabularies. These words, then, are not new to the writer. She already knows them. All she has to do is learn to spell them so she can include them in her writing as needed. Vocabulary development, the teaching of new words, should occur in the various content areas where those words are encountered in context.

How, then, do commercially-available spelling programs typically arrive at their spelling vocabulary? Beginning over 50 years ago, numerous studies were conducted for the purpose of identifying which words people included in their everyday writing, and the frequency of occurrence of those words. Word counts based on thousands of samples of writing were conducted. These studies resulted in numerous vocabulary lists, usually designated as "the 100 most frequently occurring words," "the 1000 most frequently occurring words," and so on. Even lists of "spelling demons"—words that were most frequently misspelled, were compiled.

Examination of these lists reveals considerable agreement on which words are written most often. These studies have also revealed that the 2000 most frequently occurring words in children's and adults' writing comprise about 95 percent of our writing. The spelling vocabulary for the elementary school, then, doesn't have to include thousands of words—just the **right** 2000 to 3000 words.

A basic spelling vocabulary is not included here for two reasons. First, the vocabularies of most commercially-available spelling programs are based to a considerable extent on those earlier vocabulary studies. And second, most teachers rely heavily on those programs. Thus considered, the space needed to list 2000 to 4000 words here cannot be justified.

However, in order to make an interesting point, it is appropriate to include the list of 100 spelling demons that Johnson compiled. [1] When examining Johnson's list below, note that children are typically very familiar with these words, and that the words are among those that children encounter very frequently in their reading materials. The point is, we can't assume that children know how to spell words simply because they use them in their speech or encounter them frequently in their reading.

their	said	than
to	because	two
there	thought	know
they	and	decided
then	beautiful	friend
until	it's	when
our	wanted	let's
asked	hear	sometimes
off	from	friends
through	freightened	children
mother	for	an

continued on next page

another	February	school
threw	once	you're
some	like	clothes
bought	they're	looked
getting	cousin	people
going	something	pretty
course	named	went
woman	came	where
animals	name	stopped
running	tried	very
believe	here	morning
little	many	together
things	knew	happened
him	with	didn't
it's	all right	always
started	before	surprise
that's	caught	jumped
would	every	around
again	different	dropped
heard	interesting	babies
received	swimming	money
coming	first	to
where		

Handwriting

*The ability to write words legibly, including consistency in formations, size, slant, and alignment of letters, spacing within and between words, and formatting

*The ability to write numerals legibly, including consistency in formations, size, slant, and alignment, use of punctuation marks, and formatting

Persistent common problems in manuscript writing:

*Placing the paper in the wrong position, especially the left-handed writer's fishhook position

*Holding the writing instrument in an awkward, inefficient manner

*Inconsistent slant

*Confusion of lower-case b and d, m and n, and reversal of letters, especially b, d, and s.

Persistent common problems in cursive writing:

*Placing the paper in the wrong position, especially the left-handed writer's fishhook position

*Holding the writing instrument in an awkward, inefficient manner

*Incorrect formation of lower-case a, b, e, f, i, r ,s, t, and z.

*Formation of capital letters

*Inconsistent slant in handwriting

*Connecting lower-case letters:
   *From check-stroke ending to next letter
   *From undercurve ending to down-curve beginning

continued on next page

Grammar and Usage

*The ability to include a subject and a predicate in each sentence
*The ability to make subject and predicate agree in number
*The ability to use pronouns that agree in number with their antecedents
*The ability to form and use verb tenses correctly
*The ability to use pronouns in the correct case
*The ability to place prepositional phrases in close proximity to their objects
*The ability to avoid use of certain expressions, such as *irregardless, hisself,* and double negatives
*The ability to avoid confusion of words, such as *then* and *than, to* and *too,* and *their, there,* and *they're.*

Persistent common problems needing special attention:

*Incorrect formation of past tense and past participle forms of irregular verbs
*Using pronouns in the wrong case
*Referring to self before others in compound subjects
*Double negatives
*Pronouns that disagree in number with their antecedents
*Unclear pronoun referents
*Subjects and verbs that disagree in number
*Homonyms and other words often confused, such as *then* and *than,* and *close* and *clothes.*
*Use of *at* as the last word in a sentence
*Incorrect word usages that appear most often:

Then for *than*	*Don't* for *doesn't*
Your for *you're*	*Went* for *gone*
Was for *were*	*Come* for *came*
Were for *where*	*Brung* for *brought*
Their for *they're*	*Gave* for *given*
Their for *there*	*Took* for *taken*
No for *know*	*Drank* for *drunk*
To for *too*	*Redundant pronoun*
To for *two*	
Of for *have*	
Of for *off*	
Him for *he*	
Me for *I*	
Her for *she*	
Were for *we're*	
Lets for *let's*	
Or for *our*	
Seen for *saw*	
Done for *did*	
By for *buy*	
Close for *clothes*	
Herd for *heard*	
Ran for *run*	

It is generally assumed that these charts are of value to supervisors and classroom teachers for several reasons. These charts supposedly aid the supervisor when attempting to determine if a teacher is "covering the subject matter." They are also supposed to help the teacher determine the adequacy of each child's progress and make sure no essential concept or skill is omitted.

Although such charts may be well intended and of possible value for PR purposes and for judging overall program success, there are potential risks in use of these charts. They can result in a program that is regimented and subject-oriented rather than child/learner-oriented. Teachers and administrators can become so concerned with "covering the subject matter" that they ignore or fail to take into account the fact that *each* child learns to write at *his* own pace, and that there will be a wide range of writing abilities and writing problems in a given class. Also, close adherence to the scope and sequence chart by a teacher precludes taking advantage of "teachable moments"—unanticipated opportunities to introduce something when there is a *real* need for it. For example, there may be an opportunity to introduce quotation marks to first graders in a dictated personal experience story *before* quotation marks are scheduled to be introduced. Should the teacher delay introducing this item until the prescribed time in the scope and sequence chart, or should it be introduced beforehand if a meaningful opportunity presents itself? By all means, don't miss a valuable opportunity for learning!

It should be clear, then, that appropriate uses of scope and sequence charts do not include regimentation of a program, nor should they result in a subject-oriented classroom. Properly used by the classroom teacher, they should serve as a guide for sequencing subject matter, with the teacher adjusting her expectations and introduction of learning tasks according to the needs and abilities of her students. Let's face it—ultimately, the students set the pace. Otherwise, some children will be frustrated by being expected to achieve what they cannot, while others will be bored by unnecessarily repeating tasks that they have already learned.

The sequence chart beginning on page 107 is a composite of different writing programs. It is a general outline of concepts and skills as they are *usually* introduced in writing programs. As noted above, it should not result in unrealistic expectations and "force feeding" a child certain concepts and skills simply because, for example, he is a fourth grader and those items are placed at that level. It could, however, help a teacher identify a child's developmental level as a writer, then determine what *is* appropriate for him—whether he is an accelerated student or one who is below the level associated with his age group or grade.

The Importance of Attitude

As with all learning tasks, the learner's attitude plays an important part in skill development. Poor attitudes foster poor writers. Children who are competent writers are those who believe that they are "good" writers and look forward to opportunities to write and share what they have written. It is important, then, that children develop positive attitudes about the act of writing and about themselves as writers.

Attitudes, however, cannot be taught as we would teach a skill. They are shaped indirectly and, once formed, resistant to change. Although many factors may affect formation of an attitude, the environment we create and the practices we implement at school can play a significant part in shaping a child's attitude toward writing. We can meet this challenge by (1) designing programs that are learner appropriate— based on what a child is capable of achieving and reflect his interests, (2) modeling positive attitudes, (3) employing effective teaching techniques, and (4) creating a general atmosphere that is conducive to writing—that is, writer friendly. These matters have been addressed in detail in chapters 3, 4, and 5. The BENCHMARKS OF THE WRITING PROGRAM and the ASSESSMENT OF THE WRITING PROGRAM in Chapter 4 should be of particular value.

SEQUENCE OF WRITING SKILLS

Sentence Sense

Kindergarten/Grade 1
- *Concept development: What is a (simple) sentence?
- *Sentences that tell
- *Sentences that ask

Grade 2
- *Review previously introduced items as needed
- *Expanding the simple sentence (with adjectives and adverbs)
- *Combining sentences:
    - *Two simple sentences joined by use of adjective(s)
    - *Two simple sentences joined by use of compound subject, compound predicate
- *Varying sentence beginnings
- *Saying what you mean: Word order

Grade 3
- *Review previously introduced items as needed
- *Combining sentences:
    - *Two simple sentences joined by use of prepositional phrase
- *Exclamatory sentence
- *Say what you mean: Word choice

Grade 4
- *Review previously introduced items as needed
- *Combining sentences:
    - *Two simple sentences joined by *and* , *or*, and *but.*
- *Saying what you mean: Excluding unnecessary words
- *Imperative sentences

Grade 5
- *Review previously introduced items as needed
- *Combining sentences:
    - *Combining simple sentences by use of appositive
- *Saying what you mean: Clear referents

Grade 6
- *Review previously introduced items as needed
- *Combining sentences:
    - *Two simple sentences joined by use of subordinate clause
    - *Two simple sentences joined by use of subordinate clause *and* previously introduced items

Paragraph Sense

Kindergarten/Grade 1
- *Concept development with examples in reading materials
- *Group-generated paragraph based on group experience and provided lead topic sentence
- *Organizing sentences in the paragraph

continued on next page

Grade 2
   *Review previously introduced items as needed
   *Individually-generated paragraph based on provided topic sentence
   *Writing directions
   *Personal experience paragraph with lead topic sentence
   *Imaginative narrative material, one or more paragraphs
Grade 3
   *Review previously introduced items as needed
   *Descriptive paragraph with lead topic sentence
   *Personal experience story, two or more paragraphs
   *Imaginative narrative material, two or more paragraphs
   *Organizing paragraphs in proper sequence
   *Avoiding *and so* and *and then* as sentence beginnings
   *Minimizing use of *said* to introduce quotes
Grade 4
   *Review previously introduced items as needed
   *Personal experience story, multiple paragraphs
   *Imaginative narrative material, several paragraphs
   *Using exact words rather than *nice, good, pretty, a lot,* etc.
Grade 5
   *Review previously introduced items as needed
   *Paragraph that begins with supportive sentence rather than a topic sentence
   *Maintaining point of view
   *Extended personal experience story
   *Extended imaginative narrative writing
   *Expository writing of two or more paragraphs
   *Persuasive writing, at least two or three reasons and supportive information
Grade 6
   *Review previously introduced items as needed
   *Writing material in third person
   *Writing material from different point of view
   *Extended personal experience story
   *Extended imaginative narrative writing
   *Persuasive writing, including several reasons and supportive information
   *News story of two or more paragraphs

Punctuation
Kindergarten/Grade 1
   *Period at end of sentence that tells
   *Period after numbers in a list
   *Question mark after sentence that asks
   *Comma between date and year
   *Comma between city and state, city and country
Grade 2
   *Review previously introduced items as needed
   *Commas in address
   *Comma in greeting and closing of letter

continued on next page

*Period after initial in a name
*Period after *Mr., Mrs., Ms., Dr.*
*Period when writing dollars and cents
*Exclamation mark
Grade 3
*Review previously introduced items as needed
*Period after abbreviation
*Comma in series of three or more
*Apostrophe in common contractions such as *you're, he's, we'll*
*Colon when writing time in digital form
*Hyphen with compound words
*Quotation marks for direct quote
*Comma after noun of address
* Comma to set off quote
Grade 4
*Review previously introduced items as needed
*Colon after greeting in a business letter
*Apostrophe to show possession
*Comma between two independent clauses joined by *and, or,* or *but*
*Period after numbers and letters in outline
Grade 5
*Review previously introduced items as needed
*Comma to set off appositive
*Hyphen to divide words at end of line
*Underline title of a book, magazine, movie
*Quotation marks around title of article, story, poem
Grade 6
*Review previously introduced items as needed
*Comma after dependent clause at beginning of sentence
*Colon to introduce list
*Comma to set off parenthetical or transitional expressions such as *yes, however*

Capitalization
Kindergarten/Grade 1
*First word in a sentence
*Names of people
*Names of days, months
*The pronoun *I*
*Name of school, street, town
*Title of a story
*Names of holidays
Grade 2
*Review previously introduced items as needed
*Addresses
*Greeting, closing in a letter, note
*Titles of people (*Mr., Mrs., Ms., Miss, Dr.*)
*Names of pets

continued on next page

*Names of special local places, such as a mall, river, park

Grade 3

*Review previously introduced items as needed

*First word in a quote

*Titles of books, poems

*Names of organizations

Grade 4

*Review previously introduced items as needed

**Mother, father* when not preceded by a possessive noun or pronoun

*Names of special features, such as *Grand Canyon, Golden Gate Bridge, Lake Mead*

*Names of oceans, mountains, other natural features

*Outlines

*Title of someone when used with her name

Grade 5

*Review previously introduced items as needed

*Commercial trade names

*Abbreviations in names of businesses

*All proper nouns

*Abbreviations in addresses

Grade 6

*Review previously introduced items as needed

*Proper adjectives

*Names and abbreviations of government agencies and international organizations, such as the *FBI, Organization of American States*

Handwriting

Kindergarten/Grade 1

*Manuscript:

*Paper position for left-handed, right-handed

*Holding the writing instrument

*Lower-case letters:

    Formations, shape and size, alignment

*Upper-case letters:

    Formation, shape and size, alignment

*Numerals:

    Formation, shape and size, alignment

Grade 2

*Continue manuscript learning tasks introduced earlier

*Optional: Introduce cursive handwriting. If cursive is introduced, proceed as follows:

    *Paper positions for left-handed, right-handed

    *Holding the writing instrument

    *Lower-case letters:

        *Formation, shape and size, slant, alignment

        *Connecting letters

    *Upper-case letters:

continued on next page

*Formation, shape and size, slant, alignment
Grade 3
*Recommended: Introduce cursive handwriting at beginning of school year, then follow suggested items listed above.
*Maintenance practice on manuscript as needed
Grades 4 - 6
*Maintenance practice on manuscript as needed
*Maintenance practice on cursive as needed

Grammar and Usage

Kindergarten/Grade 1
*Subject/verb agreement in number:
Using *is/are, was/were* in simple sentences
*Using *saw/seen, come/came, do/did, give/gave*
Grade 2
*Review previously introduced items as needed
*Using *went/gone, did/done, run/ran*
*Subject, predicate in a simple sentence
*Compound subject, compound predicate in a simple sentence
*Using *he/she/I* in compound subject of a simple sentence
*Subject/verb agreement: using *has/have*
*Using *a/an*
Grade 3
*Review previously introduced items as needed
*Using *ran/run, gave/given, ate/eaten, their/there/they're, your/you're, to/too/two*
*Subject/verb agreement: using *don't/doesn't*
Grade 4
*Review previously introduced items as needed
*Using *were/we're/where, of/off, then/than, brought* instead of *brung, took/taken, new/knew*
*Redundant pronoun
Grade 5
*Review previously introduced items as needed
*Using *me/him/her/them* in compound object of simple sentence
*Using *no/know, by/buy/bye, lets/let's, herd/heard, close/clothes, or/are, knew/known*
At as last word in sentence
*Avoiding *irregardless, theirselves, hisself*
Grade 6
*Review previously introduced items as needed
*Unnecessary words in sentences
*Using *have* (instead of *of*) with *should* in future perfect tense
*Using *lend/borrow, drank/drunk, grew/grown, rode/ridden, threw/thrown*
*Subject/verb agreement in sentences that begin with *there*
*Subject/verb agreement in number despite intervening prepositional phrase

NOTES

1. Leslie W. Johnson, "One Hundred Words Most Often Misspelled by Children in the Elementary Grades," Journal of Educational Research 44, no. 2 (October 1950): 154-55.

APPENDIX

FLIGHT OF THE BUZZARD
by Jerral R. Hicks

Clothes hung still from the clothesline as the afternoon sun blazed in the cloudless sky. In the distance a meadowlark called from the top of a fence post while two buzzards circled silently high above. The milk cow stood under the chinaberry tree, swishing flies with her tail as she chewed her cud. Doug, 11, Jerral, 9, and Carol, 6, brushed gnats from their faces as they sat in the wilted grass in their back yard.

"All we ever do is swim in the canal, ride our bikes, and shoot BB guns," complained Doug. "I'm tired of doin' the same things everyday."

"Me too," agreed Carol.

"We can't even fly a kite—there's no wind," added Jerral, as he raised his straw hat and wiped sweat from his forehead.

"Yeah, I already thought of that," Carol sighed.

"Doug continued to sit, just gazing into the distance, not saying a word. He then lay back into the grass, staring up at the sky as he continued to chew on a piece of grass. Suddenly, his eyes opened wide, he jumped to his feet, and shouted, "Hey, I got a great idea! Come on!" Jerral and Carol grabbed their hats, then ran after their brother as fast as their bare feet would carry them.

"What are we gonna do?" shouted Carol.

Without looking back, Doug yelled, "Just follow me! I'll show ya!" as he raced toward the shop.

As dust swirled around his feet in the shop, Doug asked, "Where'd we put those traps?"

"You mean those we use to catch coons with?" responded Carol.

"Yeah," replied Doug as his eyes searched the dusty, sagging shelves in front of him.

"They're over there," answered Jerral, pointing to rusty, twisted pile on the floor in the corner.

Doug grabbed three of the traps and a hammer, then rushed out of the shop, with Carol and Jerral chasing after him.

"But what are we gonna do?" shouted Carol.

Doug glanced back at his brother and sister and shouted, "Come on! Remember that armadillo we killed the other day? I got a great idea!"

After running far into the pasture, Doug stopped next to the dead armadillo. Puffing, Carol and Jerral arrived as Doug began untangling the traps. Flies buzzed about the swollen, rotten carcass.

Standing upwind to avoid the rancid odor, Carol frowned and asked, "What are you gonna do with that stinky ole thing?"

"Just help me put these traps around it," Doug responded. He then dropped to his knees next to the carcass and began hammering the stake of one of the traps into the ground.

"But what are we gonna catch?" inquired Carol.

Glancing up at two buzzards circling high overhead, Doug responded, "A buzzard! They oughta be comin' for a meal pretty soon."

"A buzzard? But what are we gonna do with a buzzard?" asked Jerral.

"I'll show ya later. Just help me finish puttin' these traps around the armadillo."

After placing the last trap near the armadillo, Doug advised, "Okay, let's hide in those bushes under those trees and wait for a buzzard to light."

Quietly, Doug, Carol, and Jerral lay in the bushes waiting, brushing gnats from their faces. Two buzzards circled overhead, then a third.

"Hey, look! They're gettin' lower and lower," observed Jerral.

Finally, one lit a few feet from the armadillo and cautiously began looking around, turning its wrinkled, gray head in all directions. The second and third buzzards circled lower and lower, then lit nearby. The first buzzard stepped slowly toward the armadillo, carefully checking the surroundings with each step.

"Get down so he won't see ya," whispered Doug.

It took a bite, then looked around again. Quickly realizing that the coast was clear for a tasty meal, it began hurriedly eating like a starved dog. Not wanting to miss the delightful meal, the other buzzards quickly walked over to the armadillo and began eating.

The buzzards soon began pecking at each other as they crowded closely for the tasty meal. Suddenly, one began flapping its wings as if it were trying to take off.

Carol yelled, "Hey, look how that one's hoppin' around!"

Jumping to his feet, Doug yelled, "We got one! Come on!"

Two buzzards leaped into the air. The third jumped and flapped frantically as it struggled against the chain attached to the trap on its foot.

Standing around the buzzard, Doug, Carol, and Jerral just looked at it—as it sized them up. Most noticeable was its bald, wrinkled, gray head, with a few hairs near its beak. Several dingy black feathers were twisted out of place. Its feet looked much like those of a chicken—except for their dingy, dark color. The buzzard stood motionless, occasionally blinking it round, gray eyes.

Then Carol cringed, "Ooooooh, he's so ugly."

"Now what are we gonna do with him?" winced Jerral.

"We gotta grab him and take him to the shop," responded Doug.

"Uhhhh, I don't wanna touch him. He stinks—and he's got some ole stinky stuff from the armadillo on his beak," cringed Carol.

Doug grabbed the chain and slowly began pulling the buzzard toward him as it wildly flapped its wings. He eventually managed to grab one of the buzzard's feet.

"Hold him down! I gotta get the trap off!"

After looking at each other for a moment, Jerral and Carol stepped forward and grabbed the buzzard's outstretched wings. Doug released the trap, then grasped the buzzard's legs and said, "Okay, let's go. We gotta take him to the shop."

"But what are we gonna do with him?" asked Carol with a puzzled expression on her face.

"Just follow me—I'll show ya," responded Doug. He then turned and began walking hurriedly toward the shop with the buzzard hanging from his hand.

After entering the shop, Doug said, "Okay, Carol, get one of those big spools of binder twine Daddy uses when he bales hay. I'm gonna tie on his leg."

"Hey, now I know what we're gonna do!" exclaimed Jerral.

Suddenly, Carol jumped back and yelled, "Look out! He's———ooooooh! Look at that nasty stuff!"

"Ooooooh, he's puking. He's trying to put it on us—make us let him go," cringed Jerral, as the gray, paste-like puke continued to spurt from the buzzard's beak.

"Grab his neck, Jerral, and hold his head down so he can't get it on us," ordered Doug.

"Ooooh, it stinks so bad. Don't get it on you," advised Carol from a safe distance.

Jerral hesitated, then grabbed the buzzard's neck from behind, and Doug tied the twine on its foot. Doug then picked up the buzzard and said, "Okay, Carol, get the spool of twine and follow me."

Behind the shop, Doug put the buzzard on the ground and, holding it firmly with both hands, advised, "Okay, start unwinding a lot of twine—I mean a lot!"

After unwinding about 60 feet, Carol asked, "Is this enough?"

"No, keep unwinding it—and hurry!"

After about 300 feet were unwound, Doug observed, "Okay, that's enough. Now I'm gonna let him go, so hold the spool real tight."

"Okay, I got it," answered Carol.

Doug let the buzzard go and it sat for a moment, looking around. Then, realizing it had a chance to escape, it leaped into the air, flapping its wings frantically. It seemed to leap higher into the sky with each flap of its wings.

"Wow! Look at 'em go!" grinned Jerral.

"Boy, he's really goin'!" laughed Carol.

"Look how high he's goin'!" shouted Doug. "And y'all thought we couldn't fly a kite. Just look at ...."

Suddenly, a loud voice behind them angrily demanded, "What are you kids doin'?" Douglas, Carol, and Jerral just stood there, slack-jawed and speechless. "I said, `What in the world do y'all think y'all are doin?'"

"Uhhh, we're flyin' our kite, Momma," responded Doug.

"A kite my eye! That's a filthy buzzard! Have y'all been handlin' that thing?"

"Uhhhh, well, just a-a-a little," stammered Doug.

"That's just what I thought. Those things carry all sorts of diseases. I want y'all to let that bird go and get to the house and wash your hands—now!" She then turned and walked briskly back to the house. Doug quickly began pulling on the twine to get the buzzard down.

After pulling on the twine for a few minutes, the buzzard lay exhausted on the ground with its beak open and its wings outstretched. Jerral grabbed the buzzard and held it firmly while Doug untied the twine. Then they stepped away from the bird. It looked around for a moment, then struggled back into the sky.

"Boy, that was fun," said Carol with a grin.

"Yeah, but I wonder what that buzzard thought," laughed Doug.

Doug, Jerral, and Carol looked at each other and laughed. They were right proud at having outsmarted a buzzard. Then the back door at the house slammed and the kids turned their heads toward the house. Their laughter stopped, their eyes opened wide, and Doug warned, "Uh-oh, here comes Momma with a switch!"

Jerral then looked back up at the buzzard. As he watched it fly higher and higher, he thought, "I wonder if that buzzard's laughing at us now?"

BIBLIOGRAPHY

Applebee, Arthur N. and others. Writing Trends Across the Decade, 1974-1984. Report no. ETS-15-
W-01. Princeton: National Assessment of Educational Progress, 1986.

Arbuthnot, May Hill and Shelton L. Root, Jr. Time for Poetry, 3rd ed. Glenview, IL: Scott Foresman
and Co., 1968.

Beeker, Ruth Ann. "The Effects of Oral Planning on Fifth-Grade Composition." Dissertation
Abstracts International 30, no. 11, 1970.

Bereiter, Carl and Marlene Scardamalia. "From Conversation to Composition: The Role of Instruction in a Developmental Process." Advances in Instructional Psychology 2. Hillsdale,
NJ: Lawrence Erlbaum Associates, Publishers, 1982.

Brossell, Gordon. "Rhetorical Specifications in Essay Examination Topics." College English 45, no.
2(February 1983): 165-73.

Calkins, Lucy McCormick. "Children's Rewriting Strategies." Research in the Teaching of English
14, no. 4(December 1980): 331-41.

Calkins, Lucy McCormick and Donald H. Graves. "When Children Want to Punctuate: Basic Skills
Belong in Context." Language Arts 57(May 1980): 567-73.

Emig, Janet. "The Composing Process of Twelfth Graders." ED 058 205, 1971.

Golub, Lester S. and Wayne C. Fredrick. "An Analysis of Children's Writing Under Different
Stimulus Conditions." Research in the Teaching of English 4, no. 2(February 1970): 168-
80.

Harari, Herbert and John W. McDavid. "Name Stereotypes and Teachers' Expectations." Journal of
Educational Psychology 65, no. 2(October 1973): 222-25.

Hillocks, George, Jr. Research on Written Composition: New Directions for Teaching. Urbana, IL: ERIC Clearinghouse on Reading and Communication Skills, 1986.

Hoyt, Franklin S. "Studies in English Grammar." College Record 7(1906): 467-500.

Johnson, Leslie W. "One Hundred Words Most Often Misspelled by Children in the Elementary Grades." Journal of Educational Research 44, no. 2 (October 1950): 154-55.

Kellogg, Steven. How a Picturebook is Made: The Island of the Skog. The Signature Collection. Weston, CN: Weston Woods Studios, 1976. Filmstrip/tape.

Lederer, Richard. Anguished English. 1987. Reprint. New York: Dell Publishing, 1989.

McKee, Blaine K. "Types of Outlines Used by Technical Writers." Journal of English Teaching Techniques 7, no. 4(Winter 1974/1975): 30-36.

O'Hare, Frank. Sentence Combining: Improving Student Writing Without Formal Grammar Instruction. Research Report No. 15. Urbana, IL: National Council of Teachers of English, 1973.

Schroeder, Thomas Steven. "The Effects of Positive and Corrective Written Teacher Feedback on Selected Writing Behaviors of Fourth-Grade Children." Dissertation Abstracts International 34, no 6, 1973.

Silverstein, Shel. Where the Sidewalk Ends. New York: Harper Collins Publishers, 1974.

Stallard, Charles K., Jr. "An Analysis of the Writing Behavior of Good Student Writers." Dissertation Abstracts International 33, no. 7, 1973.

INDEX

ABOUT THE AUTHOR

Dr. Hicks began his teaching career in the mid-1960s with his first teaching assignment in public schools. In 1968 he completed work for his masters degree in elementary education at Sam Houston State College, then began work on his doctorate. He completed work for his Doctor of Education degree at the University of Northern Colorado in 1970, with a major in elementary education that emphasized language arts.

During the next 13 years, Dr. Hicks served as a faculty member in teacher training programs at the university level. In addition to teaching classes in traditional elementary education programs on campus, he worked in competency-based programs and field-oriented programs off campus where he taught courses and numerous workshops in the field. He served in various supervisory roles and administrative roles, including assistant department chairman, and program development specialist and inservice coordinator in special programs. These roles provided opportunities for Dr. Hicks to observe and to evaluate a considerable variety of learning activities, program elements and strategies, and materials and equipment in classrooms.

Beginning with his earlier experiences as a student in a teacher training program, Dr. Hicks began to realize that there were serious deficiencies in children's writing. This observation was reinforced during his teaching experiences in the public schools. He also began to see first-hand the inadequacies of the treatment of written composition in traditional teacher training programs.

In response to these deficiencies in writing and the earlier admonitions of his high school English teacher, Grace Payne, to pursue a career in writing, Dr. Hicks developed a special interest in written composition. He began emphasizing written composition in the language arts courses he taught in college, and developing workshops that focused on written composition in the elementary school. He continued to refine his ideas about teaching children to write when he returned to the public schools as a language arts teacher in the 1980s.

Dr. Hicks is now devoting his time to writing about various concerns in education and serving as a guest speaker and consultant. This book is his most extensive written contribution about writing to date. It is a culmination of countless experiences as a writing teacher in public schools, as a student of his students, and as a teacher in higher education.

Jerral R. Hicks, Ed.D.
3204 Thunderbird
Las Cruces, NM 88001
September 12, 1992